# Linking and matching

D1350451

# Linking and matching
## A survey of adoption agency practice in England and Wales

Cherilyn Dance, Danielle Ouwejan, Jennifer Beecham and Elaine Farmer

Published by British Association
for Adoption & Fostering
(BAAF)
Saffron House
3rd Floor, 6–10 Kirby Street
London EC1N 8TS
www.baaf.org.uk

Charity registration 275689 (England and Wales)
and SC039337 (Scotland)

© Cherilyn Dance, Danielle Ouwejan,
Jennifer Beecham and Elaine Farmer, 2010

British Library Cataloguing in Publication Data
A catalogue record for this book is available
from the British Library

ISBN 978 1 905664 82 5

Project management by Jo Francis, BAAF Publications
Designed by Helen Joubert Associates
Typeset by Avon DataSet Ltd, Bidford on Avon
Printed in Great Britain by TJ International
Trade distribution by Turnaround Publisher Services,
Unit 3, Olympia Trading Estate, Coburg Road,
London N22 6TZ

BAAF is the leading UK-wide membership
organisation for all those concerned with
adoption, fostering and child care issues.

# Contents

## List of figures

## List of tables

## Notes about the authors

**Cherilyn Dance** is a senior research fellow in the Child and Family Welfare Research Centre at the University of Bedfordshire. Her background is in health and child development. A good deal of her research to date has concerned looked after children, much of which has focused on adoption and permanence for older children, with particular attention to the placement of siblings and support for adoptive families. Previous books on these topics include: *Joining New Families: A study of adoption and fostering in middle childhood* (1998); *Siblings in Late Permanent Placements* (2001); and *Adoption Support Services for Families in Difficulty* (2002).

**Danielle Ouwejan** worked as a research associate at the School for Policy Studies, University of Bristol, over the course of this research study. Her background is in social pedagogy and her interests include psychosocial problems in childhood and adolescence, adoption and permanence. She currently lives in the Netherlands, where she works on a small research project investigating an intervention program for Ugandan street children and orphans.

Professor **Jennifer Beecham's** research has included studies, mainly with an economic focus, on services for people with needs related to mental health, learning disabilities, and old age. Many of her projects over the past 10 years have focused on children, including evaluations of children's social care and mental health services. Professor Beecham is based at the PSSRU, University of Kent and the London School of Economics and Political Science.

**Elaine Farmer** is Professor of Child and Family Studies in the School for Policy Studies at the University of Bristol in the UK, prior to which she spent several years as a social worker in England and Australia. Her recently completed research on reunification, kinship care, neglect and adoption were funded by the Department for Children, Schools and Families. Her books include: *Trials and Tribulations: Returning children from local authority care to their families* (1991); *Child Protection Practice: Private risks and public remedies* (1995); *Sexually Abused and Abusing Children in Substitute Care* (1998); *Fostering Adolescents* (2004); and *Kinship Care: Fostering effective family and friends placements* (2008).

## Acknowledgements

We would like to express our gratitude to the Department for Children, Schools and Families (DCSF) for funding this research and providing overall support. We are especially indebted to Caroline Thomas, who has been a responsive and supportive link to the Department and who has chaired our advisory and progress meetings so well.

We are also very grateful indeed for the extremely valuable advice and support of our advisory group, our consultative group of adoption professionals and our university colleagues. Any limitations in the report, of course, remain our responsibility.

Our final word of thanks goes to the many managers in the local authority and voluntary adoption agencies who gave so generously of their time in sharing their experiences and thoughts with us in the completion of our questionnaire. We are indebted to them.

## Service provider and advisory group members

Jenny Castle, Institute of Psychiatry
Charmaine Church, Department for Children, Schools and Families
Jennifer Cousins, British Association for Adoption & Fostering
Isabella Craig, Department for Children, Schools and Families
Mary Davidson, Surrey County Council
Elaine Dibben, Department for Children, Schools and Families
Margaret Dight, Catholic Children's Society
Cherry Harnott, independent consultant
Jill Hodges, consultant psychotherapist
Karen Irving, St Christopher's Fellowship
Sylvia Little, London Borough of Lewisham
Paul McCrone, Institute of Psychiatry
David Quinton, University of Bristol
Gwen Rule, British Association for Adoption & Fostering
John Simmonds, British Association for Adoption & Fostering
Andy Stott, Adoption Register for England & Wales
Caroline Thomas, University of Stirling (Chair and DCSF academic advisor for the Adoption Research Initiative)
Shiraleen Thomas, Department for Children, Schools and Families

## The ARI series

This series brings together the research studies in the Adoption Research Initiative (ARI), a programme of research on adoption funded by the Department for Children, Schools and Families (DCSF). It is designed to evaluate the impact of the Government's adoption project, including the Adoption and Children Act 2002 and various related policy initiatives. The research initiative is examining how these objectives are being translated into local policies, procedures and practice.

There are seven studies within the Adoption Research Initiative. They address four broad themes: permanency planning and professional decision-making; linking and matching; adoption support; and the costs of adoption. They also complement other recently-reported and current research on the full range of placements for looked after children, including kinship care, foster care, residential care, private fostering and return home.

*Linking and Matching* is the second of these studies to be published by BAAF, the first being *Enhancing Adoptive Parenting*, by Alan Rushton and Elizabeth Monck.

# Executive summary

## The research

Linking and matching in adoption is the process of identifying an adoptive family which might best be able to meet the needs of a child who is waiting for an adoptive placement. More specifically, linking refers to the process of investigating the suitability of one or more prospective adoptive families who might meet the needs of a certain child or sibling group, based on their prospective adopter's reports (Form Fs). Matching refers to the process whereby a local authority decides which prospective adoptive family is the most suitable to adopt a particular child. This family will be brought forward as a "match" for the child or sibling group at the adoption panel.

Little is known about how linking and matching are approached and which models of practice are currently in use. This area has not been investigated systematically before. The survey therefore aimed to identify and categorise variations in practice and policy in linking and matching across England and Wales, and to estimate broad costs for some of the related adoption activities. The survey is the first part of a larger study on linking and matching in adoption, funded by the Department for Children, Schools and Families (DCSF) under the Adoption Research Initiative (ARI).

The survey was conducted by means of a self-completion questionnaire, which could be completed on the internet or manually between July and October 2006. A total of 168 local authorities which undertook adoption work and 29 voluntary adoption agencies were approached and of these, 44 per cent of local authorities and 55 per cent of voluntary adoption agencies agreed to participate. This response rate is broadly in line with that from other similar surveys.

## Profile of participating agencies

Analysis of the statistical information provided by agencies suggested that there was considerable variation in the proportions of children adopted by their existing foster carers (from none to over a third of agency placements), while placement with single, same-sex or disabled adopters was uniformly rare. There was considerable variation in the proportion of agencies that were able to place children with their own adopters, from some which placed all their children with adopters recruited by them to a few which placed almost all children through inter-agency means. Shire counties, in particular, were more self-sufficient in terms of being able to place children with families recruited "in-house". Respondents from many other types of local authority commented that various features to do with their geographic position or local population profile impinged on their ability to place within their own resources.

Across all participating local authorities, agency statistics showed that on average just over half the adoptive placements they made were "in-house". Placements made through consortia arrangements accounted for just over a quarter and other inter-agency arrangements secured placements for the remainder. The Adoption Register was used by the majority of agencies and was reported as being a particularly important source of links for some of the agencies, which were not readily able to place children within their own resources. On average, agencies reported inter-agency fees being payable for around 35 to 40 per cent of cases. Local authorities often proceed sequentially in their search for links, beginning with their own resources, proceeding to use families from their agency consortium if necessary and only involving voluntary agencies if they have no success with their own or local resources.

It was also interesting to find that the proportion of children placed with a sibling varied from 14 per cent to 80 per cent of placed children. Such a spread might indicate differential policies on the separation of sibling groups, or indeed on the timing of taking children into care and moving them on to adoption. Similarly, the proportion of placed children who had special health needs or disabilities was reported as varying from none to 29 per cent. This might reflect different views about the definition of a special health need or disability but equally might indicate greater determination to place such children for adoption in some agencies than in others.

## Assessment and preparation of children

There was variation in the extent and the timing of transferring case responsibility from one section of service to another. In 30 per cent of the local authorities, case responsibility for children moved to a specialist adoption or permanency team once the placement order had been made. Nevertheless, many agencies pointed out that an adoption worker was "linked" to a child's case even where the main responsibility remained with the child's social worker.

In terms of developments in this area of work, sibling assessment was frequently cited and several agencies mentioned joint working with, or opportunities to refer to, mental health specialists where necessary. Eight agencies conducted assessments of the child's attachment status and two used story stem narratives as part of assessing children's needs. (In a story stem assessment children are asked to respond to a set of story stems where they are given the beginning of a story highlighting everyday family scenarios with an inherent dilemma and their attachment patterns are assessed based on the children's responses).

In addition, a number of agencies had consultancy in place to aid social workers and others in their assessment work with children (for example, from a clinical psychologist or multi-agency team), whilst nine used a child psychologist to undertake individual assessments in complex cases.

There was also some variation as to who undertook direct work with children to prepare them for adoption. Although in the majority of cases (90%) the child's social worker would, at least to some extent, be involved in this, many agencies also mentioned the involvement of others to undertake these tasks because of time constraints on children's social workers. Agencies that delegated this task tended to refer children either to a specialist worker or to engage family centre staff or social work assistants.

## Recruitment and preparation of prospective adopters

Agencies told us that there continued to be difficulty in recruiting sufficient adopters for children with additional needs, particularly families able to consider children with disabilities, those with a black or minority ethnic background and to some extent for older children and those with special health needs. Perhaps surprisingly, about a quarter of the agencies did not appear to operate targeted recruitment drives to find families able to meet such needs. This is consistent with findings from adoption agencies' inspections (CSCI, 2006) where three out of ten local authorities and one in ten voluntary agencies had not developed strategies to recruit adoptive parents to meet the needs of children who were waiting.

The practice approaches most commonly mentioned by survey respondents were attachment style or status assessments, which were incorporated, in full or in part, into the home study phase of adopter assessment by 14 per cent of agencies. (The Attachment Style Interview (ASI) and the Adult Attachment Interview (AAI) are used to assess the attachment style of prospective adopters.) The other notable developments were in mentoring and support for prospective adopters by more experienced adopters in the preparatory phase, and the use of support groups.

## Family finding

Developing a profile for a child who needs an adoptive placement was generally the responsibility of the family-finding or adoption worker. In the majority of agencies, the worker would meet with the child before embarking on the family-finding task, but in 14 per cent of the responding agencies the child was rarely or never seen by the family finder.

Agencies exploited a variety of mechanisms to locate families for children but service level agreements were rarely used. From agencies' responses, we identified four different mechanisms for identifying links, the first two of which might be described as "professionally-led" and the latter two as "adopter-led" approaches.

i.   First-hand knowledge of a potential family assessed by the adoption team.

ii.  Links through an exchange of information between social workers or, since the establishment of the Adoption Register and some databases run by consortia, by computer.

iii. Presentation of a child's profile to the community of approved adopters by, for example, features in the *Be My Parent* or *Children Who*

*Wait* publications, "in-house" profiling events and exchange events.
iv. Presentation of a child's profile to the wider community through newspapers, radio or television features. (This approach was rarely used.)

In recent years, there have been significant moves towards the further development of adopter-led approaches. Half of the agencies in the survey had secured links through presenting the child's profile at regional adoption events or video evenings, while featuring children on the internet had provided some links for 17 per cent of agencies. Specific family-finding magazines such as *Be My Parent* (BAAF) and *Children Who Wait* (Adoption UK) had been used by over 90 per cent of the agencies, although this route accounted for a relatively small proportion of the placements made in most agencies.

## Deciding which family to proceed with

For most respondents, the highest priority factors in matching were meeting children's emotional, behavioural, attachment and health needs, in concert with the suitability of the adopters' parenting style. Other considerations, including needs in relation to ethnicity or contact, children's interests or talents and birth family wishes, while important, when set against the needs just mentioned, generally came slightly lower down the priority list.

From agencies' reflections on key factors in matching we identified four groups of issues. First there were those related to practice, processes and organisation within agencies, such as providing adequate preparation and support; not stretching adopters' preferences; ensuring that all the relevant parties worked together; and involving foster carers in adoption plans. Second, there were factors to do with the adopters' characteristics, such as their parenting skills; support networks; the likely impact on their own children; and their distance from the placing agency. A third set of considerations were adopters' attitudes and understanding of the adoptive parenting task, including their understanding of the child's history; having realistic expectations of adoption; and being comfortable with contact plans. Finally, two other issues were mentioned: "chemistry" – or a feeling of "emotional connectedness" with a particular child – and having regard to a child's views on the proposed placement. The analysis of these responses showed how matching is about balancing relative strengths and vulnerabilities and the importance of the wider context, that is, the way in which an agency operates and the experience and knowledge of the workers directly involved. However, the issue that was mentioned by far the largest number of respondents in this context was the importance of having clear and accurate information about both the child and the prospective adopters.

In looking at barriers to matching, the primary problems that respondents identified were those resulting from the attitudes of some children's social workers who kept looking for the "ideal family", difficulties in relation to the placement of siblings, contact plans and complications in adequately reflecting children's ethnic heritage in a proposed adoptive placement. One further concern, particularly raised by voluntary agencies, was finance. Several respondents felt that the inter-agency fee was frequently an obstacle to effective matching, particularly as the fee for a family approved by a voluntary agency is considerably higher than that for a family approved by another local authority.

This exploration of adoption professionals' views on matching issues also showed that there are contrasting views in the field on a number of contentious issues. These include very varied opinions on: the balance to be struck between matching on ethnicity and avoiding delay; how far contact plans should be shaped by what adopters think they can manage; how soon the matching criteria (or placement plan) need to be reviewed if no match has been found for a child; and whether adopter-led matches lead to better outcomes than those which are led by professionals. In addition, the responses highlighted the crucial role of the child's social worker in knowing the child well and the accompanying difficulties when workers changed or refused an apparently suitable match. This suggests a need for further consideration of the appropriateness of the role of the children's social worker as the final decision maker.

## The matching process
Agencies said that they would generally follow up one, two or more commonly three links at any one time, although a minority reported more. The majority of agencies followed up links primarily through discussions

with the workers for the families involved, rather than with the families themselves; but there was variation in whether the families were made aware that they were being considered for a child. The survey responses did illustrate continuing tensions around how many, and at what stage, families are approached directly to explore whether they may be able to meet a child's needs.

In terms of the matching process, in most agencies (76%), decisions about which families to proceed with were taken in a formal matching meeting. When formal meetings were not used, children's social workers (sometimes with their managers) would liaise with family-finding workers or adoption team managers in order to reach a decision. Most respondents emphasised that the "decision" about matching ultimately rested with the children's worker (or their team).

One of the survey respondents commented that matching as a task is, as yet, relatively unexplored and conceptually underdeveloped. In line with this, there appeared to be fewer developments in the matching process than in other aspects of adoption work in many agencies. Some agencies (4–5) were trying to make the matching process more systematic and objective by using a matrix or grid to compare children's and families' characteristics.

All agencies used the Child's Permanence Report along with children's medical and other assessment reports to present information to prospective families, and 85 per cent of agencies shared video or DVD images of children. Sight of the child's case file was available to families in only 55 per cent of the agencies, but all the agencies involved the foster carers and other professionals in sharing information with prospective adopters. At the time of the survey, Life Appreciation Days were being used (for some children) by 55 per cent of agencies, but many other respondents expressed an interest in developing this practice in their own agencies.

## The adoption panel

There was substantial variation between agencies in the frequency with which panels requested further information before making a recommend-ation. Before recommending that a child should be placed for adoption, further information was requested by the panel for between none and

30 per cent of cases. Panels can also refuse to make a recommendation. Agencies reported that panels refused to recommend the plan for adoption in between none and 18 per cent of their cases and that they refused to recommend a proposed match in between none and 10 per cent of cases, with this never occurring in 35 per cent and 50 per cent of agencies respectively. Data were available for relatively few of the busier panels but there was a tendency for these agencies to report a higher proportion of papers being returned with requests for further information in order to consider whether a child should be placed for adoption.

Examples of practice development in terms of working with the panel included the use of checklists and practice guidance tools to assist panel members in making their decisions, joint training for panel members with social workers, and panel members attending external courses. There was also mention of the use of feedback systems to panels from socialworkers, adopters and sometimes children, expecting panel members to come to meetings with prepared written comments, and de-briefing after meetings.

## Cost estimation of adoption activities

There is no doubt that the processes that are undertaken to place a child for adoption are both time-consuming and costly. On average, each child assessment takes 55 hours to complete over a four-month period at a cost of £2,500. Although completing the assessment form for prospective adoptive families absorbed slightly more social work time (64 hours), the average cost was slightly lower at £2,200 and took place over about six months. It is not clear why this cost was lower although it is possible that the costs of some child assessments are elevated by the use of specialists. Preparing a child's profile cost an average of £147 and took six hours to complete. Talking to children, families and professionals as part of the linking process absorbed a further three-and-a-half days, on average, at a total of £1,200. The number of hours spent on each of these activities was broadly in line with other research (Selwyn *et al*, 2006) and the average cost of the four processes amounts to over £6,100. Our work in the second stage of the research will provide further validation of the costs estimated to date as well as estimates for some other adoption-related activities, such as for adoption support in the first six months of placement, further strengthening the evidence base on the costs of adoption.

## Developing a typology of practice approaches

One of the purposes of the survey was to try to identify distinctive variations in adoption practice which might lend themselves to further investigation in terms of their effectiveness and their associated costs.

As the analysis of the survey data progressed, it became clear that there were four identifiable practice variations that were likely to be amenable to grouping for the purposes of the comparative study planned for the second stage of this project. Other variations might have been included but a larger number would have made later statistical analysis difficult. The practice variations by which we have selected agencies for the second stage of the study are:

a) the stage at which transfer of case responsibility to adoption and permanence specialists takes place;

b) utilisation of the Attachment Style Interview and the Adult Attachment Interview frameworks in the assessment of families;

c) "adopter-led" methods: that is where a variety of media are used (for example, using written profiles, children's artwork, photographs, DVDs) to introduce profiles of children needing adoption to prospective adopters. Prospective adopters are then asked to identify children to whom they feel they are likely to respond well;

d) the routine use of matching tools and formalised meetings.

## Conclusions

Overall, the survey reveals that there is significant variation in adoption practice across agencies and there is also much innovation in practice, although relatively little of it is at present directed at matching. The report highlights a number of novel ideas and developments, although very few have been subject to any evaluation. We have also identified a number of issues which were identified as obstacles to making timely adoption placements, as well as areas where there are still diametrically opposed views or that are in need of further research. Some of these questions will be addressed by the planned second stage of this research.

While it would not be appropriate to draw implications for policy or practice from this kind of survey, the results do provide an interesting snapshot of current practice in England and Wales and guidance on where attention might be focused in future research.

## References

CSCI (2006) *Adoption: Messages from inspections of adoption agencies*, London: Commission for Social Care Inspection

Selwyn, J., Sturgess, W., Quinton, D. and Baxter, C. (2006) *Costs and Outcomes of Non-Infant Adoptions*, London: BAAF

# 1 Background to the research

In order to thrive and develop to their potential, children need stability, nurturance and a relationship with a consistent and caring adult (Howe, 1995). For most children these needs will be met within their own birth families. However, a minority of families are either unable or unwilling to provide the level of care needed to parent a child adequately. Historically, many such children were found to have "drifted" in the public care system (Rowe and Lambert, 1973). Since the 1980s there has been significant interest in trying to secure permanence, stability and a sense of belonging for children by seeking adoptive families for those who cannot grow up within their own families. Research undertaken during the 1980s and 1990s showed that in many cases adoption could provide permanent families for children and that "outcomes" were often very positive (Barth and Berry, 1988; Borland et al, 1991; Quinton et al, 1998). These findings were encouraging, and in the late 1990s the aim of increasing the proportion of children placed from care with adopters was explicitly articulated in *The Prime Minister's Review of Adoption* (Performance Innovation Unit (PIU), 2000); children's services targets and performance indicators related to adoption practice were introduced rapidly thereafter. In 1999, the Government set a target for the number of children to be adopted from care to increase by 50 per cent between 1999/2000 and 2005/06. While the number of children adopted has increased markedly, this target was not in fact met, with an actual increase over the period of 37 per cent (Commission for Social Care Inspection (CSCI), 2006a).

The outcomes of adoptive placements, although measured in a variety of ways, have generally been found to be positive in terms of children's adjustment and adoptive families' levels of satisfaction (Groze, 1996; Triseliotis, 2002). However, many commentators have noted that considerable support is sometimes required (Rushton and Dance, 2002b) and that, on occasion, placements do not progress well. The likelihood of disruption (premature ending of a placement) has most consistently been found to vary according to characteristics such as the age of the child when placed with an adoptive family (the older the child, the greater the likelihood of difficulty) and the level of behavioural difficulties (Rushton, 2000). Although these factors are associated with higher rates of placement disruption, research studies have also shown that families vary in their ability to accommodate different types of behavioural problems and, equally, placements of children as old as 10 years can sometimes be very positive for the child and the adoptive family alike. Clearly, there are issues about ensuring that the correct support is available, but the first part of the puzzle has always been how best to make judgements about which families may be right for which children.

## A note about terminology

The process used by local authorities to identify adoptive families most suited for particular children is known as "linking and matching". These terms, although in common parlance, have slightly different meanings for different agencies and professionals. It seems sensible, therefore, to define the way in which we shall use them at the outset.

As used in this report, "**linking**" refers to the process of investigating the suitability of one or more prospective adoptive families who, based on their PAR (Prospective Adopter's Report, formerly Form F), seem to meet the needs of a particular child or sibling group. "**Matching**" in adoption can be defined as the process of identifying a family whose resources will, as far as possible, best meet the assessed needs of a particular child or sibling group throughout childhood and beyond (Hadley Centre for Adoption and Foster Care Studies (Hadley Centre), 2002). Put another way, it involves fitting parents' strengths to the needs of children awaiting placement (Ward, 1997). A proposed match between a child and family, although initially determined by the social workers involved, must be presented to the agency's adoption panel, which will examine the evidence for and against the match and make a formal recommendation to the agency decision maker.

## Existing research on linking and matching

Most of the descriptive data on linking and matching were collected prior to the introduction of the Adoption and Children Act 2002 (Quinton *et al*,

1998; Lowe *et al*, 1999; Owen, 1999; Rushton *et al*, 2001) and appear to reflect general assumptions about which kinds of children should be placed in which type of families. Triseliotis and colleagues (1997) concluded that: 'there is no substantive research about matching of children and families, and there are many different opinions about what is important' (p 157). The Hadley Centre's research summary on this topic reached similar conclusions (Hadley Centre, 2002; see also Parker, 1999). However, *The Prime Minister's Review of Adoption* (PIU, 2000) expressed concerns that the insistence on finding a perfect, rather than a "good enough", match was leading to delays, particularly for black and minority ethnic children; it also indicated concerns about the costs of inter-agency placements.

The current Government emphasis is on exploring permanence options, including adoption, for looked after children very early in their care careers (PIU, 2000) and, if adoption is thought to be appropriate, expediting the process of placement. The search for an ideal match will be counterbalanced by the need to meet placement targets and there is likely to be a relationship between the length of the list of matching requirements and delay in finding suitable adopters. The Adoption National Minimum Standards (Department for Education and Skills (DfES), 2003a) stress that meeting the child's needs must be coupled with avoiding unnecessary delay. The key questions are which critical needs must be met immediately and which can be met with time or with support and education for the adoptive parents. From an administrative standpoint, significant strides have been made in many local authorities to remove several of the bottlenecks in adoption procedures, in order to speed up the process and monitor progress (Rushton and Dance, 2002a). Statistics suggest that children under the age of one year are being placed within five months of the formal recommendation being made, and for older children this is being achieved on average within nine months (CSCI, 2006b).

While figures indicate that many adoptive placements are achieved relatively swiftly, failure rates following introductions and during the first year of adoptive placement are high for some groups of children (Selwyn *et al*, 2006). Yet, as indicated above, there has been very little research to date that has focused explicitly on how decisions are made about which family to choose for a child and whether better approaches to matching might reduce these failure rates (Quinton, forthcoming).

A scan of several searchable bibliographic databases (e.g. Evan Donaldson Institute, *Adoption & Fostering* articles, Social Care Online, Social Services Abstracts, Psychinfo) found that, in comparison with associated topics such as recruitment, assessment, preparation, introductions and post-placement support, the literature on matching *per se* is extremely scant. This is somewhat surprising given the importance of the complex matching process that needs to take place. Placing children, many of whom have complex needs, with an unrelated adoptive family is one of the most important decisions in child care. It is also potentially one of the most difficult. Lowe and his colleagues (1999) report social workers talking of a balancing act in trying to consider the multiple factors involved.

Despite the lack of research evidence, social work practice in relation to adoption has been developing over time and ideas about which issues should be considered in matching for adoption have varied accordingly. For example, following the Second World War, matching on looks and religion predominated (Quinton, forthcoming), whilst more recently, matching on ethnicity and culture have been emphasised (Frazer and Selwyn, 2005; Selwyn *et al*, 2008). In addition, efforts are currently made to match children's needs to adopters' parenting, or indeed "re-parenting", abilities (Archer and Gordon, 2004) in order to help children overcome early adverse experiences rather than (as previously) on simply finding a child for a family or a family for a child (Quinton, forthcoming).

We know from a variety of sources that there are a number of circumstances associated with particular dilemmas for practitioners who need to place children with adoptive families. These same circumstances are also likely to be associated with delays in placing children for adoption. Prominent among these are making decisions for black and minority ethnic children, for those with disabilities or health problems and for children who have siblings (Ivaldi, 2000; Rushton, 2000 and 2003). In relation to ethnicity, for example, in their recent study, Selwyn and colleagues (2008) concluded:

*The impetus towards ethnic matching given by recent legislation seemed to dominate social workers' and agencies' thinking on place-ments. While it is right and proper that this is high up on social workers' agendas, it seemed that the issue often dominated thinking to the detriment of meeting the child's other developmental and psychosocial needs.* (p 220)

With regard to sibling groups, there are two major issues to be considered. The first is whether related children should be placed together or separately, based on an assessment of their individual and joint needs (Lord and Borthwick, 2008). The second is whether there are sufficient families approved for sibling groups. From a comparison of the characteristics of children and adoptive families referred to the Adoption Register, it appears that it is particularly larger sibling groups, of three or more children, that are likely to be more difficult to place. According to the Adoption Register's 2007 report, there were 240 sibling groups of three children needing an adoptive family, but just 59 adoptive families able to consider up to three children. The figures for sibling groups of four children were 28 sibling groups and six families. No families at all were able to consider the five sibling groups of five children. This apparent lack of families must have an impact on how decisions are made in relation to the placing of sibling groups.

Children who have additional needs in relation to disabilities or serious medical problems are also known to wait longer for a family, and research suggests that this is, at least in part, due to a dearth of families willing to consider children with these problems (Cousins, 2005).

Traditionally, family finding has relied on marrying up adopters' preferences as indicated in a series of tick-boxes on their profile, with a similar listing of "matching considerations" on the profile of the child. More recently, this approach has been considered to be too restrictive (Cousins, 2003) and a variety of relevant initiatives have been discussed in the practice press, particularly in relation to methods of finding families for the children who are likely to be more difficult to place. These are outlined in detail by Cousins (2008) but, briefly, involve various means by which approved adopters are given an increased opportunity to see and hear about "real" children who are waiting for placement – not just in terms of what their characteristics might be, but also to discover more about the "whole child". Many of these approaches build on developments pioneered in the UK in the early 1980s by staff from the voluntary adoption agency Parents for Children.

Although specific research evidence is scarce, there are several general texts on matching and aspects of practice pertinent to it (BAAF, 1998; Hadley Centre, 2002; DfES, 2003b; Harnott and Humphreys, 2004). These tend to emphasise the importance of factors such as realistic expectations on the part of prospective adopters, allowing an opportunity for them to express doubts as well as enthusiasms, and – especially – encouraging children to express their views about an adoptive placement and listening carefully to what they say. Recommendations such as these arise from research studies that have sought adopters' views of the preparatory phases retrospectively, and also owe much to reports from practitioners who have shared their experiences of supporting placements.

When discussing the rather more elusive characteristics of children and parents, it is necessary to consider how such subtleties can be assessed, reported effectively to adoption panels and highlighted in the descriptions and profiles available for linking purposes. In an important article, Cousins (2003) argues for an overhaul of the process of assessing prospective adopters and the current linking and matching procedures, calling for fewer tick-boxes and instead working to a model that focuses on preparing families with the "real child" in mind. She also proposes a two-stage process of approval, whereby initial approval would be given without strict criteria as to suitable types of children. She suggests that this would release the adults from the anxieties associated with the panel decision and allow them to explore more openly whether particular children might fit with their family. Such a move might address some of the concerns expressed by adopters in the study by Lowe and his colleagues (1999), who experienced doubts as to whether the child with whom they were matched was the right child for them.

Millard Veevers (1991) discussed the process of matching some years ago from the viewpoint of transactional analysis, stressing that, although certain major factors needed to fit, reams of factual information about child and family did not necessarily help to match children's needs and families' qualities. What was needed, in her view, was more information about a child's psychological and emotional needs and whether families could provide for these.

Writing from a United States perspective, Gerstenzang and Freundlich (2006) also draw attention to the tensions surrounding the basis on which decisions are made about which family.

*The wisdom of matching children and families on specific criteria has been the subject of great debate. Proponents of matching families and children on the basis of particular characteristics emphasise "goodness of fit" and the importance of these factors in placing a child with the right family (or placing the right child with a family). Other professionals, however, disagree. They point out that many biological children do not share the interests and talents of their parents, and that biological siblings, although often sharing some common interests and talents, have talents and interests of their own. These professionals see the prospective parent's commitment to parenting as the overarching criterion.* (p 9)

Citing work conducted by Avery in 1999, which explored the circumstances of children who had been waiting a long time for an adoptive family, these authors also draw attention to the potential role of practitioners' values and beliefs. Avery's findings suggested that beliefs about the likelihood of finding a family and beliefs about the sort of family who would suit were both important factors in the process.

A final issue that is important in terms of background to the topics covered in this report is that of the inter-agency fee. Currently, in the UK, adoption agencies recruit, assess, prepare and approve couples or individuals to become adoptive parents. Both local authorities and voluntary adoption agencies are involved in this aspect of practice. Local authorities alone have responsibility for the children who need placements and, when they have no suitable families within their own "pool" of approved adopters, will seek to place children with a family that has been approved by another agency. This is particularly likely to occur if children have more complex needs. Although various arrangements exist between agencies within consortia about payment of fees, in principle placement of a child with a family from another agency incurs a fee. Furthermore, the fees are currently set in such a way that families approved by a voluntary agency incur a higher one-off payment than families approved by another local authority. This factor has been, and continues to be, the subject of much debate since there is a perception that local authorities may be reluctant to incur the additional costs associated with inter-agency placements and that this is likely to result in delays in finding placements. A recent report commissioned by the Department for Children, Schools and Families (DCSF) found that, when all the relevant costs are properly taken into account, the inter-agency fee does not represent poor value for money and that, in fact, voluntary agency fees represent good value for money because they tend to provide placements for children with more complex needs (Selwyn *et al*, 2009).

Overall, there are a number of interrelated elements to be taken into account when discussing linking and matching and there are many ideas about how things might be done better. However, despite the high level of practice interest in this area, to date there has been little exploration of which models of linking and matching are currently in use or evaluation of whether one style of practice might be superior to another in terms of benefits to children or adoptive families. Nor have there been any attempts to "cost" systematically the different practice approaches. At present, we know very little of the thinking within agencies about the relative priority given to different sorts of needs, and whether this varies across agencies. Nor do we know what factors are perceived to obstruct or facilitate the linking and matching process, or what mechanisms may have been put into place in an attempt to enhance the efficiency or accuracy of linking and matching. Likewise, the extent to which the values of professionals are thought to be influential in the decision-making process is currently unclear and there is a need to discover whether there are differences between agencies in their preparedness to incur the costs associated with inter-agency placements. It is these gaps in knowledge that this study attempts to address.

# 2    Design and methodology

This adoption agency survey comprises the first stage of a larger research study entitled *An Investigation of Linking and Matching in Adoption*, funded by the Department for Children, Schools and Families (DCSF). The overall aims of the study are to explore variation in practice and policies related to linking and matching across England and Wales, to compare these in terms of outcomes and costs, to identify the indicators of a good match and to suggest ways in which matching might be improved. The survey sought information about and views on linking and matching practice, principally from one respondent (usually a senior adoption manager) in each local authority and voluntary adoption agency in England and Wales.

## Aims of the survey

The main aim of the survey was to identify policies, practices and decision-making processes in linking and matching children to prospective adopters at national level, and to explore the resources used to do this work. On the basis of the survey data, the research review being conducted by Quinton (forthcoming) and information about agencies using innovative approaches, we aimed to develop an initial classification of approaches to linking and matching. This would inform the selection of eight to ten agencies for the second stage of the study. In sum, the objectives of the survey were:

- to identify variations in policy and practice in linking and matching in adoption at national level;
- to estimate broad costs for some adoption activities;
- to identify categories of variation in adoption agencies' work in this area.

## Methods

### Instrument development

The method chosen for the survey was a self-completion questionnaire since the national scope of the study made alternative forms of data collection too costly and time consuming. The questionnaire itself was developed in consultation with a group of service providers, mainly adoption managers and consultants from both local authority and voluntary adoption agencies. Their input proved invaluable; we discussed how the latest developments in legislation were being implemented within their agencies as well as the impact of these changes on agency procedures. Apart from this provider group, feedback on more general issues concerning the questionnaire and the conduct of the survey was given by an advisory group consisting of academics, policy makers and practitioners.

In line with the aims of the survey, the questionnaire had to be designed to enable us to distinguish variations in linking and matching practice. Hence, one of the key tasks was to identify the areas in which variation might be expected. Clearly, identifying appropriate links for a child will be informed by the outcomes of assessment: the more thorough the assessment reports, the more information will be available to those identifying and recommending links and matches. Equally, recognition of, and provision for, support needs may enhance the likelihood of finding families. For this reason, we decided to include not only questions specifically about linking and matching but also about other contiguous areas of practice: the assessment and preparation of children and of prospective adopters, the operation of adoption panels and support services.

Because one of the aims of the survey was to explore the resources needed for different practice approaches, it was necessary for the questionnaire to include a series of questions on team composition and expenditure, time spent on linking and matching, and time spent on some of the main adoption activities. This information was requested alongside requests for broad information on the number of children approved for adoption, adoptive parents recruited, as well as placements made and disruption rates. Social workers usually find it hard to identify "typical" or "average" amounts of time spent on the various adoption activities because the children and families they support are all different. Our approach was, therefore, to ask about time spent on the last case. This would generate a sample of cases dealt with by all the agencies during the survey period.

Finally, there was a series of statements that aimed to elicit views on some of the more controversial issues in linking and matching, reflecting differing approaches and attitudes to matching priorities.

In summary, the survey questionnaire included the following sections:

- working with children who should be placed for adoption;
- working with families who wish to adopt;
- linking and matching;
- the adoption panel;
- the adoption team;
- statements (reflecting the views and experiences of respondents).

In each section, we asked for factual information about the way in which agencies approached the task under investigation, but also provided opportunities for agencies to describe any aspects of their practice or any developments they felt were in any way unusual or innovative. Of course, what is considered unusual or innovative by one person may be thought of as routine by another; we were therefore exercised by how to phrase these questions to ensure we captured as much innovation as possible. Our eventual choice was to ask, 'Does your agency use, or have you developed, any particular tools or approaches in working with . . .'. The question was cumbersome but we hoped that this phrasing would maximise the number of respondents who felt they could answer the question and therefore provide us with examples of practice developments and innovation.

## Finalising the questionnaire and method of delivery

Before being sent out, the questionnaire was piloted, which enabled us to identify problems with either the format or the content. The pilot led us to revise certain questions and the sequence of presentation (see the example below) but it also showed us that the electronic version of the question-naire (originally developed using Microsoft Word) was not user friendly and did not function in the way we had planned. We therefore started looking for another solution to formatting the questionnaire.

The comment below was received at the pilot:

> . . . as in most large local authorities, specific information, such as financial, is held centrally. Therefore, I am entirely in their hands in terms of if and when they complete their questions.

This led us to gathering all the financial questions into one section, so that delays due to passing the questionnaire on to colleagues would be reduced to a minimum.

Although the team agreed that respondents should have the possibility of completing the questionnaire by hand, there were good reasons to stimulate electronic completion: it allowed respondents to edit and amend their answers, it could be reproduced easily and data entry was more efficient and accurate.

In searching for a reliable method of on-screen completion, we were attracted to the Bristol Online Survey (University of Bristol). There were a few important advantages to using an online survey. First, both qualit-ative and quantitative data could be exported directly into a database. Second, since the survey was online, it could be completed from any computer with an internet connection, which made it easily accessible and transferable between colleagues.

## Ethics

The study gained the approval of the Ethics Committee of the School for Policy Studies at the University of Bristol and the Association of Directors of Social Services (ADSS), now the Association of Directors of Child-ren's Services (ADCS). Information about the survey was sent initially to directors of children's services and chief executives of voluntary adoption agencies, and any refusals were respected. The major ethical issue faced in this part of the study related to the tensions between maintaining confidentiality and acknowledging contributions. There has been some debate in the literature in recent years about people's preferences regarding their contributions to research being recognised (Grinyer, 2002). Because we hoped to identify good practice – and would anyway wish to acknowledge the time and commitment of respondents – we asked in the questionnaire whether people would consent to their agencies being named. Almost all of the agencies agreed to this and these contributing agencies are listed in Appendix A.

## Sample

At the time of the survey, we were able to identify a total of 173 individual local authorities and 33 voluntary adoption agencies. However, we learned that there were five local authorities whose adoption services were provided by another agency and four voluntary agencies that were not involved in placement activity. Our potential sample was therefore 168 local authorities and 29 voluntary adoption agencies.

The survey period ran between July 2006 and September 2006 (extended to 29 October 2006). Efforts were made to encourage participation by means of periodic email and telephone contact with non-respondents. A short item was also published in *BAAF News* (a newsletter produced by the British Association for Adoption and Fostering (BAAF)).

## Response rates

Overall, data were available for a total of 74 of the 168 local authorities (44%) and 16 of the 29 voluntary agencies (55%).

At first glance, the response rates might be considered a little disappointing. However, other research studies utilising self-completion survey methods in children's services and education report a mixed experience in terms of return rates. For example, a survey of children and young people receiving personal social services achieved a 28 per cent response rate (DfES, 2005). The *General Teaching Council's Survey of Teachers* (National Foundation for Educational Research, 2004) realised returns from 44 per cent of their sample, while just 23 per cent of schools responded to a questionnaire survey of schools, support staff and teachers (Blatchford *et al*, 2006).

Surveys of services specifically for looked after children have been undertaken before. Rushton and Dance (2002b) achieved a response rate of almost 70 per cent, but in this case data collection was undertaken using telephone interviews rather than postal questionnaires. More recently, Sellick (2007) reported a 63 per cent response rate in their survey of adoption support services. Conversely, BAAF's Finding Families for Children (FF4C) project achieved return rates of 25, 41 and 29 per cent for the local authority, voluntary adoption agencies and independent foster care providers surveys respectively (BAAF, 2005a, 2005b and 2005c). In their recent review of commissioning in adoption, Deloitte (2006) obtained a 70 per cent response rate from local authorities (16/23 – clearly, this did not include all local authorities in the country) and a 58 per cent response rate from voluntary adoption agencies (18/31).

We would, of course, have liked a higher proportion of agencies to participate in the study. However, our response rate, which meant that about half of adoption agencies were represented, was broadly comparable with other similar surveys and better than some. In the course of chasing for responses, we detected a lot of interest in the study in principle and found that a number of potential respondents declined because their agency was undergoing reorganisation or inspection, or had severe staff shortages or a change of adoption manager. Overall, we feel that the level of response reveals considerable dedication and enthusiasm among many adoption personnel. This is especially so given that the questionnaire went out over the summer, was time consuming to complete, needed to be completed by someone at operational manager level, and frequently required the attention of another respondent within each agency to provide financial data.

While in theory the questionnaire could have been shortened by narrowing the focus, this would have gone against the views of our service provider and advisory groups. It also would have impacted on our ability to address questions that were central to the aims of the survey and the remainder of the research study.

## Response bias

Overall, our response rate secured the views and experiences of almost half of the adoption agencies in England and Wales, which was encouraging in view of the length of the survey. In order to consider how representative and robust the data were, we scrutinised it for indicators of response bias.

We were interested in exploring whether there might be bias in terms of geography, administrative arrangements, number of children in care or the volume of adoption work within agencies. For English and Welsh local authorities, comparative data were available to allow us to test for bias between agencies that responded and those that did not. Comparable data were not available for voluntary adoption agencies. We found some differences in the pattern of responses between English and Welsh local authorities, and for this reason we present the analyses separately for the two.

## English local authorities

By using the local authority tables produced annually by the DCSF, we were able to establish that participation rates for English councils varied between 35 and 60 per cent according to region and administrative type, but the variations were not statistically significant. Participation was highest among shire counties (60%) and lowest in outer-London boroughs (35%).

There were no significant differences between participating and non-participating agencies in terms of the number of children looked after, but there was some indication, historically at least, of more children being placed for adoption by participating agencies.[1] Figure 2.1 illustrates how participating agencies have, on average, placed more children for adoption than is the case for non-participating agencies over the last four years, although the gap between the two groups has narrowed over time. This

---

[1]  Differences between participating and non-participating agencies in rates of placement for adoption were significant in 2003 ($F = 7.9$, df $= 1.134$, p<.01). The difference in 2004 was not significant ($F = 2.9$, df $= 1,132$, p $= 0.091$), nor were differences in 2005 or 2006.

narrowing gap is largely accounted for by a reduction in the numbers placed by participating agencies and, in fact, the difference between the two groups is only statistically significant for 2003.

*Figure 2.1*
**Mean number of children placed between 2003 and 2006 by participating and non-participating local authorities (LAs), England only**

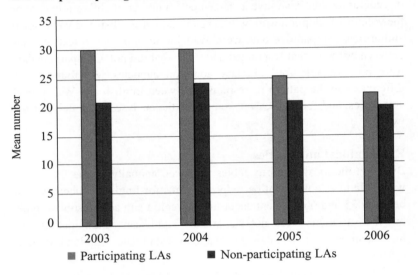

As a final measure, we examined participating and non-participating agencies for their rating on the CF/C23 performance indicator for 2005/06 (CSCI, 2006a). This indicator is published as a "rating" on an annual basis by the DCSF and is calculated from returns made by local authorities in England. The rating is arrived at by application of the following formula:

*The number of looked after children adopted during the year as a percentage of the number of children looked after at 31 March (excluding unaccompanied asylum seekers) who had been looked after for six months or more on that day.*

In 2006, children leaving care under a special guardianship order were also included in these figures (CSCI, 2006a). The result of this check is displayed in Figure 2.2,[2] which shows the range of ratings for each of the two groups. The two plots are almost identical, suggesting no bias within our sample in terms of current performance in relation to the proportion of children adopted from care.

*Figure 2.2*

**Proportion of looked after children adopted in 2005/06 for participating and non-participating English local authorities (LAs)**

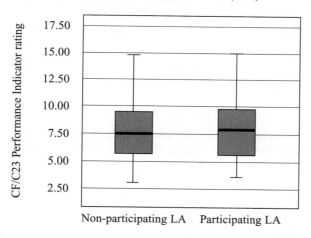

Given that our participating agencies were placing slightly more children in earlier years than was true for non-participating agencies, it is possible that participating agencies had rather more experience on which to draw but overall, we can be reasonably confident that our sample was broadly representative of practice across England.

---

[2]   Boxplot: The box itself contains the middle 50 per cent of the data. The median is indicated by the solid black line in the box. The horizontal ends of the vertical lines show the minimum and maximum data values, and any points outside of these are outliers or suspected outliers (see Appendix D).

## Welsh local authorities

The picture for Welsh agencies was somewhat different. First, positive responses to the survey were received from only 22 per cent of Welsh agencies. Looking back over publicly available data from recent years, we could detect no systematic differences between non-participating and participating Welsh agencies in terms of the number of children they looked after, nor indeed the number or proportion of children placed for adoption during the 2003–2005 period (Local Government Data Unit, 2007). In common with the picture for England, a graphic illustration of the mean number of children placed for adoption by participating and non-participating agencies (see Figure 2.3) immediately draws attention to the fact that, on average, participating agencies were placing children more frequently. These differences were not statistically significant, although they may appear substantial because of the relatively small number of agencies involved in the analyses.

*Figure 2.3*
**Mean number of looked after children adopted in 2005/06 for participating and non-participating Welsh local authorities (LAs)**

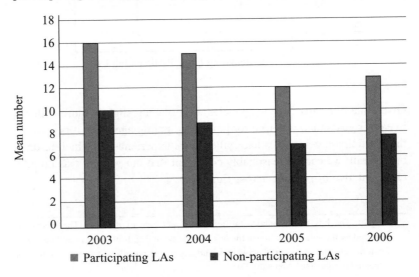

Upon examining figures for 2006, however, we found marked differences in the proportion of looked after children adopted from care, according to agencies' participation status (see Figure 2.4).[3] These differences were statistically significant, although some caution is needed due to the small group sizes. Where group sizes and indeed the populations involved are small, it is quite feasible for relatively small changes in circumstance to have a disproportionate impact on statistics. But taken overall, these analyses suggest that the Welsh agencies that engaged with this survey may have been more actively promoting adoption for a longer period.

*Figure 2.4*
**Proportion of looked after children adopted in 2005/06 for participating and non-participating Welsh local authorities (LAs)**

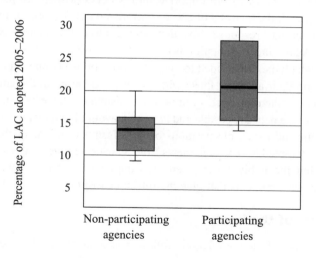

---

[3] Differences in adoption activity between participating and non-participating agencies were tested using ANOVA (a statistical procedure used for comparing mean (average) values on a continuous scale across two or more samples (or groups)). For the numbers of children adopted, $F=6.75$, $df=1,20$, $p<.02$. For the proportion of looked after children adopted, $F=12.75$, $df=1,20$, $p<.01$.

## Analysis

Numeric data from the questionnaire were entered into SPSS, a software package for the statistical analysis of quantitative data. Analyses are descriptive for the main body of the report, principally using frequencies and cross-tabulations. Wherever statistical significance was tested, a probability of less than 0.05 was regarded as significant: meaning that where any association is described as "significant", the likelihood of such a relationship occurring by chance was less than one in 20. Unless otherwise stated, categorical data were subjected to the chi square test (or Fisher's exact test two-tailed, where appropriate) and continuous data were tested using analysis of variance (ANOVA: a statistical procedure used for comparing mean (average) values on a continuous scale across two or more samples (or groups)).

Free text responses were imported into NVIVO (a software package that assists with the analysis of text or narrative data). We used it to help us group similar responses together and explore the themes which emerged. Again, the presentation is descriptive. Participants varied in the extent to which they responded to open questions or used opportunities to elaborate on their answers; those who did respond varied in the compre-hensiveness of their answers. In presenting this material, we have tried to be as true to the data as possible and have endeavoured to indicate whether excerpts are individual observations or are illustrative of major themes. We have attempted to represent views from as wide a range of agencies as possible but inevitably, where there was duplication of ideas, we have elected to use comments that give the fullest description.

## Structure of the book

The remainder of the book largely follows the sequence of the question-naire, focusing first on the context in which adoption services are delivered in different agencies: the structure and function of the various social work teams, for example, and the volume of adoption activity. This is followed by an examination of arrangements for the assessment and preparation of children and adoptive families, an essential precursor to effective matching. Chapter 6 explores *linking*, which we define here as the process of finding families that *may* meet a child's needs. Chapters 7,

8 and 9 move on to consider *matching*, which is used in this report to denote the process of comparing the relative strengths and needs of both children and families to produce a match between a specific family and an individual child or sibling group. This section forms the bulk of the report, relying heavily on views provided through open commentary. In Chapters 10 and 11, we explore the operation of adoption panels and identify the cost implications of adoption teams and some of the activities they undertake. Our conclusions draw together the main findings from the survey, setting them in a policy and practice context.

## Terminology

There are a number of terms and phrases used in this report that are very specific to the field of adoption of looked after children. We have therefore provided a glossary of the more unusual terms in Appendix B. Explanatory footnotes are also used on occasion.

## Summary

- The survey used a self-completion questionnaire that was developed in consultation with a group of adoption professionals. Most respondents used the online version of the questionnaire.
- The questionnaire covered methods of assessing and preparing both children and families for adoption, linking and matching procedures, the operation of the adoption panel and elements of information required for cost estimations.
- The potential sample included a total of 168 local authority adoption agencies and 29 voluntary adoption agencies. The survey achieved an overall response rate of 46 per cent.
- There were no substantial differences between participating and non-participating agencies on most dimensions, although for both English and Welsh local authorities there were some indications that levels of adoption activity may have been higher historically among participating agencies than was true for non-participants.

# 3   Sample characteristics

In the overall sample, 80 per cent of respondents represented local authorities and just under 20 per cent responded on behalf of voluntary adoption agencies. As illustrated in Figures 3.1 and 3.2, there was a reasonable spread in terms of both regions of the country and administrative type of authority.

*Figure 3.1*
**Distribution of agencies according to regional categories**

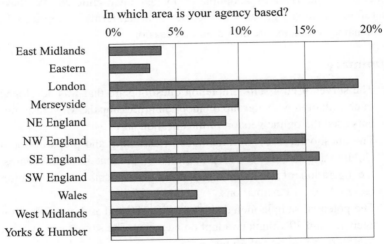

The agencies responding to this survey varied in terms of the size of population they were serving. The smallest local authority represented in the survey was looking after just 70 children and young people in 2005/06, while the largest cared for 1,360. Rates of placement for adoption in the year 2005/06 showed a similar range, with a minimum of five children placed in one authority while, at the other end of the scale, another agency had made 85 placements. Interestingly, there was some

*Figure 3.2*

**Distribution of agencies according to administrative categories**

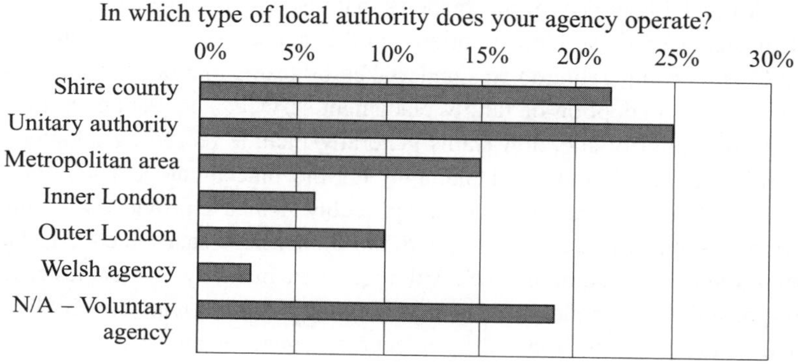

In which type of local authority does your agency operate?

discrepancy for several authorities between the number of placements reported to us and the numbers recorded in DCSF statistical reports.

## The adoption teams and organisation of services

Given the range in terms of population sizes, it is not surprising to discover that the size of social work teams dealing with adoption work varied in a similar way. Local authority adoption teams ranged from 4.5 full-time equivalent (fte) staff to 67 fte, while team sizes in voluntary agencies ranged from 2.5 to 43 fte. For local authorities, the size of teams was strongly correlated with the size of the total looked after population and the number of children placed for adoption, but was not correlated with the proportion of looked after children adopted from care (the CF/C23 indicator[4]). Thus the size of teams, in local authorities at least, seemed to be determined by the volume of adoption activity, with larger number of children needing adoption leading to a greater number of staff

---

[4] This is the number of looked after children adopted during the year as a percentage of the number of children looked after at 31 March (excluding unaccompanied asylum seekers) who had been looked after for six months or more on that day. This indicator is published annually by the DCSF.

in the adoption team; but larger teams did not necessarily suggest a greater proportion of looked after children being placed for adoption.

Around 70 per cent of the agencies that responded to the survey had a dedicated team to work on adoption. In other agencies, family-finding for children needing adoption was undertaken by teams that provided a joint fostering and adoption or family placement service. The responsibilities of local authority adoption teams generally include recruiting adopters, family finding, linking and planning for the placement, and adoption support. Many of these teams would probably also have provided consultation to social workers working with children whose cases needed to be submitted to the adoption panel. Although in the majority of agencies case responsibility for children who need adoption remains with the children and families teams, some 30 per cent of agencies reported that case responsibility transferred at the point of the care order or placement order to the more specialist adoption team.

Within these various arrangements, we wanted to know how much time was given to linking and matching children and families. Perhaps surprisingly, we found that this was reported as varying substantially. This

*Figure 3.3*

**Proportion of time spent on linking and matching children in own agency to (any) prospective adopters (dedicated adoption teams only)**

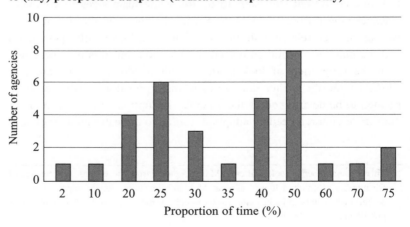

variation in the amount of time spent on linking and matching activities did not seem to relate to the size of teams, the way agencies organised adoption work or to the number of children placed for adoption. It seems likely that respondents interpreted this question in different ways, for example, having to decide whether writing a Child's Permanence Report was, or was not, part of "linking and matching".

Even when we examined only those agencies with dedicated adoption teams (see Figure 3.3), the range of responses was rather unexpected. Our categorisation of "dedicated adoption teams" was based on respondents indicating that 100 per cent of the team's time was spent on adoption-related activities. With hindsight, it might have been useful to request more information. For example, thinking for a moment about those who reported greater proportions of time, it may be that some of these teams did not focus on all aspects of adoption-related work: recruitment, for example, might be undertaken by a separate specialist team, freeing up more time for linking and matching activities.

Similarly, adoption support work might have been undertaken by a separate team or outsourced. Another possibility is that some agencies included a considerably wider range of activities in their response to this question than others. Further detail on the activities of teams represented in the survey is provided in Chapter 9, where we consider these against the costs of providing services.

## Volume of adoption activity

We asked agencies to supply some statistical data to provide a context for the volume of adoption activity within each agency. We had hoped these data would be easily extractible from the annual adoption agency reports. We were particularly interested in exploring areas not routinely covered by the SSDA903[5] return to the DCSF, such as the proportion of children placed with ethnically matched adopters, the number of children placed as part of sibling groups and the proportion of placements made through

---

[5] SSDA903 are the statistical returns for children looked after by local authorities in England, as collected by the DCSF.

consortia or other inter-agency arrangements. To this end, we asked agencies to provide aggregate data on the number of children placed and families approved during the year ending March 2006. We also asked for an indication of the numbers of both children and families involved according to a variety of specific characteristics.

A number of agencies did not provide these data at all and, for those that did, there was a degree of confusion about how to respond to some of the questions, rendering the data less than reliable. We have taken the opportunity to present the data that seemed most reliable, primarily because such information has not previously been available. However, we would emphasise that this should be interpreted cautiously and be considered indicative only. Data about matching on ethnic background characteristics have had to be excluded as they were not sufficiently reliable to report.

## The number of children placed for adoption
The variation in the volume of adoption activity among our participating agencies is well illustrated when we consider that local authorities placed between five and 96 children in the target year. Not surprisingly, shire counties tended to place far more children than their geographically smaller counterparts.

## Sibling group placement and special health needs or disability
Table 3.1 presents the ranges, means and standard deviations for the numbers of children and sibling groups placed and the proportion deemed to have special health needs or a disability. As might be expected, the correlations between these variables were substantial. According to the information supplied, agencies varied considerably in the proportion of children with special health needs or disabilities placed (from none to 29%) and in the proportion of children placed as part of a sibling group. Although the proportions clustered around a midpoint of 40 per cent, the range ran from 14 per cent to 80 per cent of children being placed for adoption with a sibling. Because numbers were small we were not able to explore these variations in more depth.

*Table 3.1*

**Numbers and proportions of children placed with siblings or with a special health need or disability (n = 35)**

| | Range | Median | Mean | SD |
|---|---|---|---|---|
| **Total children placed for adoption April 2005–March 2006** | **5–96** | **21** | **27** | **21.9** |
| Children placed with a sibling | 2–45 | 8 | 10 | 10.0 |
| Sibling groups placed | 1–21 | 4 | 5 | 4.6 |
| *Proportion of children placed with a sibling* | *14–80%* | *40%* | *41%* | *16.0* |
| Number of children with special health needs or disabilities | 0–10 | 2 | 2 | 2.0 |
| *Proportion of children with special health needs or disabilities* | *0–29%* | *8%* | *10%* | *7.6* |

## Sources of placements

We also looked at the means by which placements had been identified. Six agencies responding to this section of the survey had succeeded in placing more than 90 per cent of the children placed in the preceding year with adoptive families recruited through their own agency. Indeed, two agencies had achieved this for all of the children placed. At the other end of the scale, five agencies placed fewer than 10 per cent of children with their own adopters and one agency reported inter-agency placements for all the children it placed. Table 3.2 illustrates the frequency with which other sources of families were used and provides an indication of how often inter-agency placement fees were incurred.

As can be seen, although there is substantial variation, on average just over half the placements made were in-house, placements made through consortia arrangements accounted for just over a quarter and other inter-agency arrangements secured placements for the remainder. Nine per cent of placements were adoptions of children by their existing foster carers. Agencies reported up to one-quarter of the placements being achieved

*Table 3.2*
**Proportion of placements made through different resources (n = 34)**

|  | *Range* | *Median* | *Mean* | *SD* |
|---|---|---|---|---|
| Proportion placed with own adopters | 0–100% | 56 | 54 | 31.0 |
| Proportion adopted by existing foster carers | 0–36% | 8 | 9 | 8.4 |
| Proportion placed through consortia | 0–100% | 19 | 27 | 27.8 |
| Proportion placed – other inter-agency means | 0–68% | 27 | 28 | 17.8 |
| Proportion placed through Adoption Register link | 0–25% | 0 | 4 | 7.2 |
| Proportion for whom inter-agency fees paid | 0–100% | 35 | 39 | 25.7 |

through a link identified by the Adoption Register. On average, inter-agency fees were payable for around 40 per cent of cases.

Numbers were too small for further analysis but there are definite indications that shire counties were much more likely to be able to achieve their placements in-house, while unitary agencies seemed least able to do so. This may be because of the smaller size of most unitary authorities and the competition for families from adjoining authorities. The experience of metropolitan boroughs seemed quite mixed. The other administrative categories of agency were insufficiently represented to draw any implications from the data. Of course, making inter-agency placements need not require excessive financial outlay, depending on arrangements for sharing placements within consortia. However, shire counties reported needing to pay inter-agency fees in 0–35 per cent of cases (mean 18%) in the financial year 2005/06, while for other types of agency the range was 20–100 per cent (mean 46%). We shall return to the issue of inter-agency fees in Chapter 6, where we explore linking practice in more detail.

## Types of adoptive placements

In recent years there has been increasing acceptance of the suggestion that people who are single, those with a disability or those who are in same-sex relationships may be just as able to meet children's needs as are families who conform to the more traditional image of adopters, i.e. relatively affluent, often child-free, married couples.

We therefore tried to investigate the proportion of placements made with non-traditional adoptive families: adopters who were single or disabled, same-sex or mixed ethnicity couples. Even fewer respondents completed these questions, so the following is indicative only. As illustrated in Table 3.3, placements with single adopters or same-sex couples were a relatively unusual occurrence for many agencies and placements with adopters who have a disability were extremely rare. The proportion of children placed with black or mixed ethnicity families was rather more varied and is likely to depend on the characteristics of the children needing placement.

*Table 3.3*

**Proportion of placements made according to type of adoptive family (n = 28)**

|  | *Range* | *Median* | *Mean* | *SD* |
|---|---|---|---|---|
| Proportion placed with single adopters | 0–23% | 5.2 | 6% | 4.7 |
| Proportion placed with disabled adopters | 0–4% | 0 | 0.3% | 0.95 |
| Proportion placed with same-sex adopters | 0–14% | 0 | 3% | 4.7 |
| Proportion placed with at least one black/minority ethnic adopter | 0–66% | 11.1 | 13% | 15.6 |

## Work with prospective adoptive families

### Approving adoptive families

We were also interested in exploring the levels of approval, matching and placement activity within agencies from the point of view of the prospective adopters. On this side of adoption work, voluntary agencies are also active and we present findings for local authorities and voluntary agencies separately. First, we sought to establish the number of adoptive families approved by the agencies in the year ending March 2006. The numbers reported ranged from 0 to 81 adoptive families approved. For local authorities, the number of families approved was strongly correlated with the number of children looked after, the number placed for adoption and the size of the team ($r = 0.876$, $0.842$ and $0.883$ respectively and $p<0.001$ in all cases). The averages were very similar for local authorities and voluntary agencies (just over 20). However, there was a marked difference between shire counties, which approved an average of 40 families each, and other types of local authority, where an average of just ten families were approved in the year. The average for voluntary agencies was around 18, although with quite a wide range. This figure is very similar to that reported by Ivaldi (2000) in his examination of voluntary adoption agency activity.

One of the surprises from this section of the questionnaire was the variation noted in agencies' responses to our question about the outcome of enquiries about adoption. We asked, 'What proportion of those expressing an interest in adoption proceed to become approved adopters?' The answers ranged from 10 to 90 per cent, with quite an even spread between the two extremes. The average for local authorities was around 25 per cent of enquiries compared to about 50 per cent for voluntary agencies. In thinking about the extent of the variation, it may be that respondents interpreted the question differently, perhaps varying in the point at which they consider or record expressions of interest. Alternatively, there may be very real differences in the way that agencies respond to and counsel enquirers.

## Finding children for families

Although the reason for approving families for adoption is to provide a pool from which suitable adopters might be selected for individual children, there is some responsibility on agencies, having approved a family, to assist them in fulfilling their hopes in a timely fashion. To this end, we were interested in exploring how matches were identified from the families' perspectives. We asked agencies to indicate how many adopters had been matched with a child in the target year and, for local authorities, whether families had been matched with children from their own agency or not. Agencies reported having matched between one and 64 families. On average, seven in ten adopters had been matched with children from the same agency. Again, however, there was a marked difference between shire counties and other local authorities, with the former matching their own adopters to their own children in 75–100 per cent of cases (average 92%), while other types of agency managed to achieve this for only 60 per cent of their adopters, on average. Child-specific recruitment of adoptive families accounted for between five and 25 per cent of all families approved in the target year.

In relation to the time waiting for a match, local authorities reported an average of 60 per cent of their approved adopters being matched within six months of approval, compared to a figure of 40 per cent for adopters approved by voluntary agencies. There were no differences in the speed of matching according to the administrative type of local authority.

Given the current interest in adopter-led approaches, we were interested in the proportion of matches that might be described by agencies as "adopter led" – that is, where the initial link was initiated by the prospective adopters rather than by professionals. The responses suggest this is not yet a very common practice. Local authorities overall reported between none and 30 per cent of matches originating in this way, with an average of about 5 per cent (although one local authority reported 50%). Voluntary agencies reported an average of 20 per cent, with a range of 0–50 per cent.

Our final questions in this section related to placement disruption. Although there is debate in the literature, particularly in the United States, about the correct terminology for placement disruption (Festinger, 2002), we relied on the broad understanding of the term disruption to indicate a premature placement ending, whether before or after an adoption order. Statistical information about disruption has not been made available on a national basis. Despite a longstanding recognition of the need for it, the only source of data to date has been rates reported by individual research studies which have, of course, frequently examined specific groups of children rather than whole cohorts. We therefore asked respondents to tell us, to the best of their knowledge, how many children placed by the agency had experienced a disruption of their adoptive placement in the last three years.

This question was relevant only to local authorities and the number of usable responses to this question was very small (only 34 in total). Overall, agencies reported between none and 25 disruptions over the previous three years. There was a significant positive correlation between the number of children placed for adoption and the number of disruptions reported ($r = 0.744$, $p<0.001$). By estimating the number of children placed over the three-year period, we were able to calculate an approximate disruption ratio for each agency that varied between none and 13 per cent (mean = 4%). Comparable evidence concerning breakdown rates for all adoption placements is surprisingly scarce. Certainly, placements of older children are known to be more likely to disrupt, with 7–27 per cent of placements of school-age children ending prematurely across a number of studies and with placement disruptions occurring in between none and 6 per cent of placements of pre-school children – again, across a range of studies (Triseliotis, 2002). Very little information is available about placements that end following the granting of an adoption order.

The figures presented here concerning disruption must be treated with caution, not only because of the small number of responses, but also because agencies may not be aware of disruptions that occur following the granting of an adoption order.

## Key findings

- About 70 per cent of local authorities reported that their adoption service was provided by a dedicated adoption team. The proportion of time reported as being spent on linking and matching activity was found to vary substantially, although this may be due to varying interpretations of the question.

- Thirty per cent of agencies reported that case responsibility transferred to the adoption team at the point of the placement order or care order.

- Statistical information was provided by a relatively small number of participating agencies and must therefore be treated with caution.

- There was significant variation in terms of how placements were secured. Across all the local authorities, agency statistics showed that on average just over half the adoptive placements they made were in-house. Placements made through consortia arrangements accounted for just over a quarter and other inter-agency arrangements secured placements for the remainder. The great majority of agencies reported using the Adoption Register and this was an important source of links for some. On average, agencies reported inter-agency fees being payable for around 40 per cent of cases.

- There was considerable variation in the proportion of agencies that were able to place children with their own adopters – from some who placed all their children with adopters recruited by them, to a few who placed almost all children through inter-agency means. Shire counties not only placed far more children than other categories of local authority, but also were much more likely to be able to place children within their own resources and therefore less likely to need to fund inter-agency placements.

- Exploring the characteristics of families, the representation of single adopters, disabled adopters and same-sex couples was very low among most agencies. The proportion of black or mixed ethnicity families was much more varied and probably reflected, in part, the local population and therefore the proportion of black and minority ethnic children awaiting adoption. There was considerable variation in the proportions of children adopted by their existing foster carers (from none to over a third of agency placements).

- The proportion of placed children who had special health needs or disabilities was reported as varying from none to 29 per cent. This might reflect different views about the definition of a special health need or disability, but equally might indicate greater determination to place such children for adoption by some agencies than others.

- There was a surprising amount of variation in the proportion of children placed with a sibling (from 14 to 80%). It is possible that agencies operate different priorities and policies in terms of decision making and care planning in this area.

- The number of adopters approved by agencies varied in line with the size of their looked after population, the number of children placed for adoption and the size of the adoption team.

- Agencies reported between 10 and 90 per cent of people enquiring about adoption proceeding to become approved adopters.

- Adopters approved by shire counties were more likely to be matched with children from the same agency.

- The estimated average disruption rate, calculated from agencies' reported figures, was 4 per cent (range 0–13%).

# 4 Assessment and preparation of children

This chapter focuses on the work that is done with children for whom the plan is adoption. Sixty-three local authorities provided information on this issue. Voluntary adoption agencies did not need to respond to this part of the survey as they do not hold case responsibility for children. Percentages in this chapter were therefore calculated using the responses from 63 local authorities.

## Case-holding responsibility

A children's social work team or a children and families team usually had the main responsibility for children's cases. In 30 per cent of the agencies, case responsibility for children was transferred to a specialist adoption or permanence team once the care order or placement order had been made. Many agencies pointed out that an adoption worker was linked to a child's case when the plan was for adoption, even if the main responsibility remained with the children's social worker. The role of the adoption worker was then to give advice and guidance to the child's social worker throughout the adoption process. Whether or not a child's case should be transferred to a specialist adoption worker once the plan has changed to adoption is still quite a controversial subject. It can be argued that specialist adoption workers know the field better and that delays in family finding will be reduced due to the experience of the workers. However, transferring a case inevitably means that the new worker will not be very familiar with the child and his or her background:

*The policy of some agencies to transfer children's cases to another social worker after the care (or placement) order is granted is disastrous: it means that the social worker who visits linked families often has no knowledge of the child/ren.* Voluntary agency

The concern about this practice that leads to social workers being new to a case does, however, need to be considered in the context of staff turnover in children's social workers in general, which might very easily mean a new social worker being allocated to a case anyway (Local Government Association, 2009). A recent study (Selwyn *et al*, 2008) showed that changes in children's social workers meant that more than a third were themselves new to the child's case before the research interviews.

## Moving on to adoption

Before the plan for a child changes to adoption, agencies should have assessed the possibility of a child returning home or living with other birth family members. Ninety-five per cent of agencies reported using a form of parallel planning: that is, where the plan is reunification, but at the same time the elements of planning for an alternative permanent placement are put in place in case the plan to return home is unsuccessful. In addition to parallel planning, 16 per cent of the agencies used a concurrent planning model. This is a specialist form of parallel planning where specific carers agree to work for a time-limited period towards returning the child home, on the understanding that if this plan fails, the same carers will adopt the child (Monck, 2001).

Once adoption becomes the plan, the child's case will be presented to the adoption panel for a recommendation that the child should be placed for adoption. To make this recommendation, the panel will consider the Child's Permanence Report (CPR, formerly Form E in England; CAAR (Child Adoption Assessment Report) in Wales – for brevity, we have referred to this as the CPR throughout), which agencies compile in line with the Adoption Agencies Regulations (2005). As this document forms the primary source of information for the adoption panel and often also for prospective adopters, we wanted to look at possible variations in this area of work.

The CPR includes (Smith *et al*, 2006):

- information about the child and his or her family;
- a medical report;
- the wishes and feelings of the child and birth parents;
- contact needs;

- an assessment of the child's emotional and behavioural development and needs;
- an assessment of the parenting capacity of the child's parent or guardian;
- a chronology of the decisions and actions taken by the agency with respect to the child;
- an analysis of the options for the child's future care that have been considered by the agency, and why placement for adoption is considered the preferred option.

BAAF publishes a template for the CPR that is widely used: indeed, the majority (88%) of agencies responding to this survey used the BAAF format of the CPR.

The CPR was compiled by the child's allocated social worker in 86 per cent of the agencies. In the remainder, the main responsibility for completing the CPR was held by a specialist adoption worker or was shared between the child's social worker and the adoption worker.

In sum, we can see that there is relatively little variation in practice at this early stage of the adoption process. Statutory responsibility for the child rests, on the whole, with the child's allocated social worker, who is usually based in a child care team of one sort or another and this worker is generally responsible for completing the CPR, which forms the main part of the assessment process. Where children's cases are transferred to a specialist team, this tends to take place after the initial assessment stage and after the adoption panel has made a recommendation that the child should be placed for adoption.

For the purposes of later analyses, we grouped the agencies according to whether there was any adoption or permanence specialist input into the preparation of the CPR and whether a specialist team took responsibility either before or after the granting of a placement order. As illustrated in Table 4.1, in nearly two-thirds of agencies there was no formal involvement of adoption or permanence workers in the preparation of the CPR and responsibility for case management remained with the children's social work teams after the granting of a placement order. There were ten agencies in which a specialist adoption or permanence worker was either responsible for, or involved in, the production of the CPR (rows 2 and 4 of the table) and in six of these agencies the case would also transfer to a specialist adoption or permanence team. In 12 agencies a specialist team routinely became involved after the granting of a placement order. Overall, there was some sort of specialist adoption worker involvement in just over a third of the agencies.

*Table 4.1*
**Level of adoption/permanence team involvement**

|  | Number | Proportion |
|---|---|---|
| No adoption/permanence involvement in CPR and no transfer to adoption/permanence team | 40 | 64% |
| Adoption/permanence involvement in CPR but no transfer to adoption/permanence team | 4 | 6% |
| No adoption/permanence involvement in CPR but transfer to adoption/permanence team later | 12 | 20% |
| Adoption/permanence involvement in CPR and transfer to adoption/permanence team | 6 | 10% |
| **Total** | **62** | **100%** |

## The time taken to assess children's needs

We wanted to explore how long the process of assessing a child for adoption might take. We asked agencies to estimate how long it took to assess a child, taking the last child they had assessed as an example. A subsidiary question sought to establish whether this had been a "particularly complex" case. Figure 4.1 below illustrates the degree of variation in response to this question. For the agencies that responded to this question by describing a "routine" case, the median was 35 hours, with the hours ranging from six to 120 (N = 23). Only eight respondents described a case that was complex. The median for those cases was 49.5 hours but with a range from 15 to 200.

There was quite a substantial variation in response to this question. In discussions with a number of social workers and practitioners, it has become clear that the number of hours spent on assessing a child's needs in an adoptive placement can vary hugely, depending on the complexity

*Figure 4.1*
**How many hours did it take to assess this child?**

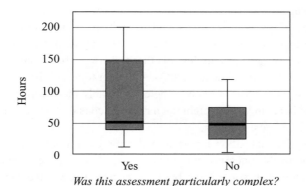

*Was this assessment particularly complex?*

of the child's history and circumstances. It is also likely to vary according to how long she or he has been looked after by the authority, how much assessment work has already been done and how thoroughly, as well as how well, the social worker knows the case. That said, there was a non-significant tendency in this sample for agencies that transferred cases from a children's team to an adoption/permanence specialist team after the placement order to report longer assessment periods than agencies where responsibility remained with the children's team (means were 66 and 37 hours respectively). The agencies in which cases were routinely transferred were not more likely than other agencies to report on complex cases. This suggests that the process of transfer, which inevitably means the involvement of a new worker, may result in a longer period of assessment.

## Particular tools and approaches: assessing children

When agencies were asked whether they used any particular tools or approaches for the assessment of children, 47 per cent of local authorities said they did. This question provided an opportunity for agencies to describe any aspects of their service in this area that they felt were particularly good or innovative. Overall, some 32 agencies indicated that they used or had developed particular approaches for assessing children's needs, although we cannot be sure that this question captured the entirety of practice.

Of the 32 agencies that responded, eight mentioned only generally available tools to assist social workers in making their own assessment. The most common examples of these were "sibling checklists" – mentioned by 18 respondents (64%) – and other tools published by BAAF. The use of these tools is likely to be considerably more widespread than suggested here since they might not have been considered to be innovative by all respondents.

The major innovation reported in the survey in relation to assessing children's needs concerned the involvement of child psychologists. This was mentioned in some form by 19 agencies. Twelve agencies had in place formal opportunities for social workers to consult with either individual child psychologists or multidisciplinary teams (one mentioned a consultation arrangement with Family Futures[6]) and seven agencies stated that these professionals were attached to their adoption teams. Other agencies mentioned referral of children for psychological assessment when this was felt to be needed. Agencies wrote, for example:

*Social workers have access to a multi-agency panel where they can discuss and gain advice about a child's placement needs.* Shire county

*The adoption team has a child psychologist attached to the team to offer advice at all stages of a child's journey to adoption.* Metropolitan area

*. . . sometimes we ask for a psychologist's assessment to ensure we understand and can meet the child's long-term needs.* Metropolitan area

---

[6]  Family Futures was established in 1998 in order to develop a specialist service for children in adoptive families, foster families and families living with children who have experienced separation, loss or early trauma. Family Futures also offers a wide range of training programmes, seminars and workshops for therapists, social workers and parents, and has produced various books and videos (see www.familyfutures.co.uk/).

The responses of eight of these 19 agencies emphasised the importance of assessment in gaining an accurate understanding of a child's attachment needs; four agencies stated explicitly that these assessments were carried out by a psychologist or other specialist and one respondent said they were part of a 'multi-professional attachment project'. A further two agencies reported specifically on the use of Story Stem narratives (Hodges *et al*, 2003) as part of assessing children's needs.[7]

> *There is a multi-professional attachment project which carries out assessments of children with complex needs. The project advises the child's carers and continues to work with them and the child, post-placement and post adoption order.* Shire county

> *For older children, the community CAMHS* [Child and Adolescent Mental Health Services] *team is increasingly undertaking a Story Stem assessment of the child, which is used to identify their understanding of the world so that we are able to inform adopters about this.* Metropolitan area

In sum, although similar concerns are evident across agencies, the approaches taken to address these vary substantially.

## Particular tools or approaches: preparing children for adoption

To prepare children who have been approved for adoption, agencies use a variety of tools. Most agencies mentioned the use of books and games in direct work with children. BAAF has published a number of books that are commonly used. Two agencies said they used a computer programme in their direct work with children, but did not specify which programme.

Direct work with children is undertaken not just by children's social workers, although they are almost always involved in the preparation of

---

[7] Story Stem narrative is a method of assessing young children's perceptions of their family and other key relationships (Bretherton *et al*, 1990). The technique has been developed by a team based in London for research use with children in transition to adoption (Steele *et al*, 1999a; Hodges *et al*, 2003).

children for adoption (90%). The vast majority of agencies also involve the foster carers (92%):

*We have produced our own children's guide to adoption, which is given to all foster carers who are caring for a child who has been approved for adoption.* Unitary authority

Twenty-nine agencies involve a specialist worker within the agency to prepare children for adoption. This could be, for example, a worker who has specialised in life story work[8] (Shah and Argent, 2006; Ryan and Walker, 2007) or staff trained to do therapeutic work with children. Occasionally, a child psychologist or play therapist would be involved. We do not have detailed information on the nature of this work as respondents did not elaborate much on their answers.

*Our therapists use an eclectic range of approaches to undertake specific preparation work for children with complex needs.* Shire county

In contrast, some agencies reported involving social work assistants and unqualified social workers to assist in undertaking preparatory work with a child. One agency explained:

*Social workers often comment on the amount of time needed to complete this work* [preparing a child for adoption]. *Social work assistants are often brought in to assist where appropriate.* Shire county

There is a view in the field that the critical elements of this work are: being reliable; having the time; and having the experience of working with children. Unqualified workers who have the experience and time may, therefore, be seen as "as good", if not better than, qualified workers who may frequently have to break appointments because they must deal with a crisis.

---

[8] Life story work is a process in which facts about a child's life are gathered to help the child understand his or her past and come to terms with it. This will help the child to move on to future placements and enable the child to speak about his or her life. As a result of this work, a life story book is usually produced which includes photos, text and, more recently, audio or video files illustrating the child's journey through life.

Relatively few agencies provided an estimate of the time needed to prepare a child for adoption, but we noted a remarkable range in the responses of those who addressed this question. The answers ranged from 'ten hours approximately' to '75 hours per child minimum'. The extent of preparation work required will depend very much on the characteristics of individual children: that is, their age, level of understanding and previous experiences. However, the complexity and sensitive nature of the work in some cases is well illustrated by the comment below:

> *It requires hours of dedicated work to prepare children for adoption. They have to understand their past in order to be able to commit to an adoptive future. A recent case of a seven-year-old took six months to prepare. It was only then the child was free to explore the idea of a new family, once she knew that she was not returning home . . .* Shire county

## Key findings: variation in practice

In addition to the use of well-known tools from, for example, BAAF, some agencies reported more innovative approaches in undertaking the assessment and preparation of children for adoption. This was more evident in the area of assessments of children than it was in relation to the preparation of children for adoption.

### Variation in the area of children's assessments

- **Consultation service for workers**: A team of experienced workers or a psychologist is available for consultation on a range of issues around planning for permanence, specifically to aid social workers in their assessments of children's needs. This approach was mentioned by 12 agencies.
- **Individual assessments undertaken by a specialist**: A clinical psychologist is occasionally brought in to undertake the assessment of a child's needs. While individual practitioners may be very experienced and knowledgeable about children's social and emotional development, in general it might be assumed that children seen by a child psychologist – or similar professional – will be very thoroughly

and objectively assessed. Other agencies reported the following, more specific forms of assessment by a specialist:

- **Sibling assessment**: This form of assessment is usually carried out to answer the question: 'Should these siblings be placed together or separately?' Many agencies (18) mentioned the use of 'sibling checklists', and it is likely that this tool is more widespread than suggested by the survey. For the purposes of this research, we have therefore considered this approach as qualitatively different to routine assessment only when undertaken by a specialist. Two agencies specifically mentioned sibling assessments undertaken by a specialist.

- **Attachment assessment**: This is usually undertaken by a specialist in cases where there is concern about a child's attachment status. This approach was mentioned by eight agencies. Assessing a child's attachment status is a fairly recent approach that is increasingly used in adoption work. Failure of affectionate relationships is one of the predictors of placement disruption (Quinton and Selwyn, 2006) and a full knowledge of a child's attachment needs may be crucial in family-finding and matching.

## Variation in the area of preparing children for adoption

- Although the amount of time agencies spent on preparation seemed to vary widely, the main variation in approach was in bringing in people other than the child's social worker to undertake this work.

- There was a contrasting approach as to which type of professional undertook preparatory work, if it was not the child's social worker. Occasionally, a child psychologist would be involved, whilst in other agencies life story work was routinely done by a worker who specialised in this area. In contrast, some agencies reported that social work assistants undertook preparatory work. These developments might be a result of the pressure on social workers' schedules, as sufficient time is needed for working with children.

# 5 Recruiting, assessing and preparing prospective adopters

Both local authorities and voluntary agencies work with people who wish to adopt. In total, 76 agencies responded to this section, of which 59 were local authorities and 17 were voluntary agencies. Percentages used in this chapter therefore represent a proportion of these 76 agencies.

## Recruitment – an agency's resource

*The successful recruitment of new adoptive parents can be considered as the sine qua non of adoption policy. This will be necessary in order to increase the pool of families from which to choose to facilitate matching and in order to achieve the government's targets for an increase in the number of children adopted from care.* (Rushton, 2003, p 17)

Undoubtedly, recruitment of suitable adoptive families is crucial to an agency's ability to place children. There are a number of factors affecting recruitment and the survey did not aim to explore agencies' strategies or practice in this area. However, it was considered important to establish agencies' perceptions of their own resources, that is, the pool of adopters from which they could select suitable families for particular children.

Many adopters initially look to parent very young white children, which creates a mismatch between the kinds of children awaiting adoptive placements and the pool of adopters. For example, in the year 2006 to 2007, just 18 per cent of adopters on the Adoption Register[9] were "black or dual heritage", whereas 29 per cent of children waiting for adoption were from a black or minority ethnic background (Adoption Register for England and Wales, 2007).

---

[9] The Adoption Register for England and Wales is a service operated under the auspices of BAAF. It is a central database for holding brief profiles of both adoptive families and children waiting for a placement. For more detail, see the Adoption Register for England and Wales website:www.adoptionregister.org.uk.

Children with certain background characteristics or special needs are often harder to find a family for and have to wait much longer than others before a suitable match is made for them (Ivaldi, 2000). This is true, for example, for children over five years old, sibling groups, children from black or minority ethnic (BME) backgrounds, and those with special health needs or a disability. In some cases, the children will eventually remain in long-term foster care because finding an adoptive family proves impossible. Perhaps not surprisingly, over 95 per cent of the agencies responding to the survey did not have an adequate pool of adopters to offer a considerable choice of families for BME children, children with

*Figure 5.1*
**Do agencies have an adequate pool of adopters to choose from for children from each of these groups?**

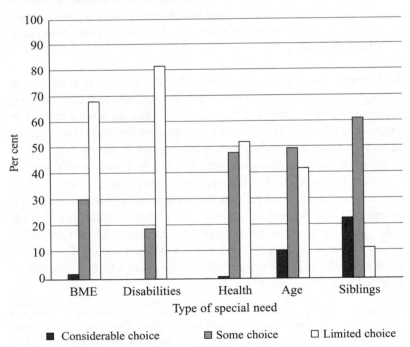

disabilities or children with special health needs (see Figure 5.1). Ninety per cent of the agencies reported not having an adequate pool of adopters for older children. For sibling groups, the situation was slightly better: 76 per cent of the agencies had only some or very little choice, whilst 24 per cent reported a considerable choice of prospective adopters for sibling groups.

Although it is clearly difficult to find adoptive families for BME children, or those with disabilities or special health needs, about a quarter of the agencies said they never specifically recruit adopters for these groups of children. In fact, 15 agencies *consistently* said they had a limited choice of adopters but *never* used targeted recruitment campaigns for any of these three groups (i.e. older children, children of BME backgrounds or children with health problems). For a few of these agencies, this may be explained by the fact that they had very small volumes of adoption work or very small BME populations in their areas. However, there was no indication in the data that agencies' recruitment practices varied consistently according to the number of children placed. In contrast, some agencies used a wide range of recruitment methods, as is illustrated in the following quotation:

> *Recruitment is ongoing and includes press adverts, recruitment displays at libraries, leisure centres, community centres, supermarkets and public events, radio interviews, targeting doctors' surgeries and infertility clinics with information about the adoption services of the agency (posters, leaflets, etc), sending information for inclusion in church magazines, Yellow Pages and adverts across the region. The agency has a comprehensive website, which is updated regularly. The agency has a team of volunteer "appealers" who promote the need for adoptive parents.* Voluntary agency

## Preparation and assessment of prospective adopters

Every adoption agency offers preparation courses for prospective adopters as a precursor to assessing their suitability to adopt. Details about the prospective adopters, the agency's assessment and other relevant information are put together in the Prospective Adopter's Report and sent to the adoption panel for consideration. The adoption panel makes a recommendation as to whether the prospective adopters should be approved or not, based on their assessed ability to provide a stable home for a child. Finally, the agency's decision maker needs to ratify this recommendation in order to approve the adopters officially.

## Particular tools or approaches: preparing and assessing prospective adopters

We asked agencies if they used or had developed any particular tools or approaches in preparing and assessing prospective adopters. Overall, 42 per cent (32 of 74) of agencies said that they did. A fair number of agencies reported the use of tools that are generally available and therefore could be considered by other agencies as relatively standard. Examples include:

- BAAF publications or publications by other organisations (e.g. *Making Good Assessments, Preparing to Adopt, Bridget's Taking a Long Time* (mentioned by seven agencies);
- tools from the *Framework for Assessment of Children in Need and their Families*, especially the HOME Inventory (Department of Health *et al*, 2000).

Other approaches that are likely to be more widespread than suggested by the responses were, for example:

- additional training for prospective adopters on specific subjects, such as domestic violence, sexual abuse and contact (mentioned by five agencies);
- getting adopters to keep a "learning log" during preparation and assessment (mentioned by four agencies);
- development of own tools within the team, shared amongst staff through a "toolkit" or an "index" of available assessment tools (mentioned by eight agencies).

Most of the tools described were aides to following up the requirements of the Adoption Agencies Regulations (Reg.24 and Sched.4 part 1). A few agencies, however, described approaches that seemed to go above and beyond the regulations. The most common example of this was the use of the Attachment Style Interview (ASI) (Bifulco *et al*, 1998) and the Adult Attachment Interview (AAI) (George *et al*, 1985; Steele *et al*, 1999b). Both interviews can be used to assess attachment style in fostering and adoption, but they use different methods. Whereas the ASI focuses on the interviewee's access to, and use of, support and current experience of confiding relationships (Bifulco, 2006), the AAI explores the ways in which interviewees recall childhood experience to inform a judgement about adult attachment status. Critically, although the AAI has an established evidence base, it is acknowledged to be difficult and time consuming to interpret (Farnfield, 2008), and the training required to code the interviews is intensive and, therefore, expensive. In contrast, there is a version of the ASI that has been developed specifically for adoption and fostering, and training in its use is nationally available. In this survey, one or other of these instruments was used by nine agencies. Five agencies used the ASI, two used the AAI and two agencies used both. Some agencies were clear in stating that the skills required to administer these measures were available within their adoption teams; others stated that they relied on external professionals, such as clinical psychologists, to provide the relevant reports. There were also one or two other respondents who mentioned using parts of these instruments or the thinking behind them.

*We use the thinking behind the Adult Attachment Interview, which has been demonstrated to have direct relevance to children's capacity to make progress in placement, e.g. develop secure attachments with their new parents, improved emotional wellbeing, improved school performance.* Voluntary agency

If we include the agencies that mentioned adult attachment without further explanation or used the ASI partly or by untrained workers, we find that 11 of 76 responding agencies (14%) showed an interest in the use of attachment theory in work with prospective adopters. Of course, agencies that do not use formal attachment inventories will, nonetheless, generally apply knowledge from attachment theory (see, e.g. Howe, 1995; Schofield and Beek, 2006).

Only one local authority mentioned the use of a concurrency

planning[10] team at this stage, although earlier in this report, findings suggested that 16 per cent of agencies use some form of concurrent planning. Naturally, this requires a specific form of assessment as the carers need to be trained and approved to act as both foster carers and adopters.

Many agencies mentioned the involvement of experienced adopters in the preparation process for prospective adopters, for example, in the *It's a Piece of Cake?* training (Mulcahy, 2000; Evaluation Trust and Hadley Centre for Adoption and Foster Care Studies, 2007), or in general support groups that continue after matching. Two agencies (both local authorities) had implemented a system where prospective adopters could be linked with experienced adopters *before approval* in order to explore and discuss specific issues, for example, in the case of single adopters, same-sex couples or families wanting to adopt a sibling group.

Finally, at a service level, one agency had implemented an approach to assessing prospective adopters that they felt made assessments more thorough:

*All assessments are co-worked by two social workers from the perm-anence team, from the initial visit onwards. We think we are fairly unusual in this approach but are committed to this way of working. We feel it results in a more thorough assessment and given the complex needs of many of the children who need adoption – and the importance of ensuring that prospective adopters are suitable for the task – we feel this is the best way of doing it.* Unitary authority

To conclude this section, we would like to give two examples of child-specific training. Although they do not fall into the same category as the

---

[10] Concurrent planning is a specialist form of parallel planning where babies and toddlers are placed under fostering regulations with carers who are approved as both foster carers and prospective adopters. The child remains with these carers while efforts are made to reach the primary goal of family reunification. During this period, the child has regular contact with the birth parents. If reunification fails, the child remains with the same family and the plan is formally approved as adoption.

other approaches mentioned – since the match will have been made already – they qualify as examples of good practice:

*Once a child is identified* (i.e. linked with one of the agency's families) *but prior to placement we offer a training session for the adopters and their support network. We consider the child's needs in terms of attachment and behaviour management. We explain these and offer strategies for the individual child.* Voluntary agency

*In some cases we have been involved with a project called "connected for life" . . . This results in foundation days where adopters can meet with a number of birth family members to gain information and, in particular, photographs and videos. A memory box is produced for the child.* Metropolitan area

## Prospective Adopter's Report

When prospective adopters are approved, their Prospective Adopter's Report (formerly Form F) becomes available to social workers who want to match a particular child to a family. As the report is the main source of information about prospective adopters, we wanted to find out whether there was any variation in how it was compiled. According to the Adoption Agencies Regulations 2005, the report should include the following (Smith *et al*, 2006):

- information about the prospective adopters – their family history, capacities, income, home and wider family, as specified in Schedule 4 part 1;
- medical adviser's health summary;
- any local authority information;
- any observations on counselling, CRB checks and preparation;
- the agency's assessment of suitability to adopt;
- any other relevant information.

As with the Child's Permanence Report discussed earlier, over 97 per cent of agencies responding to the survey used a format for the Prospective Adopter's Report that has been developed by BAAF.

Just under a third of the agencies said they used a competency framework in their assessments of prospective adopters. We offered an opportunity for respondents to elaborate on this question and although only one agency did so, the response may suggest why the use of this approach is relatively low.

*We also use the Family Centres to give four sessions to prospective adopters, both input on parenting as well as direct observation of responses to children . . . We find the Family Centre Assessment at the end of the home study a useful tool to give evidence of interaction with children. About 75 per cent of our families are childless, so we have not found the competence framework helpful.* Shire county

On average, producing the Prospective Adopter's Report took about 62 hours (N = 66, SD = 29, range = 16–170). Agencies were asked to give the number of hours the last case took, and to indicate whether this case was particularly complex or not. Strangely, the agencies describing a

*Figure 5.2*
**Number of hours needed to produce the Prospective Adopter's Report**

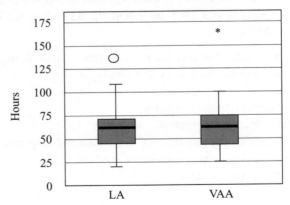

*Is your agency a local authority (LA) or a voluntary adoption agency (VAA)?*

complex case (N = 11) reported an average of 54 hours, while those describing a non-complex case (N = 55) reported an average of 64 hours. However, since only 11 agencies reported on a complex case, we cannot make any assumptions based on this difference. There were no indications of any difference between voluntary agencies and local authority adoption agencies in terms of the time taken to complete assessments, as can be seen in Figure 5.2. (The open circle and the asterisk shown above the boxes in Figure 5.2 illustrate that one local authority and one voluntary agency provided estimated hours that were substantially higher than the rest of their group.)

## After approval

Most voluntary agencies (60%; nine of 15) referred adopters to the Adoption Register straight away, whereas most local authorities (85%; 45 of 53) referred adopters three months after approval. Similarly, in 60 per cent (nine of 15) of the voluntary agencies, adopters were free to conduct their own search for a child immediately after approval, compared to only 20 per cent (eight of 39) of local authorities. For local authorities, the more usual timescale was that adopters were asked to wait for three months after approval before looking more widely, or it was said to depend on the individual case. Obviously, the majority of local author-ities first wish to explore the possibility of placing children for whom they are responsible with families that they have approved. The timescales used by most local authorities before families are referred are therefore not surprising.

When a potential link had been made for adopters, 70 per cent of agencies routinely informed their adopters about each link, but 30 per cent would not. From discussions with a group of adoptive parents – whom we consulted about the second stage of the study – we learned that being told about every potential link is not always the preferred option because of the disappointment that inevitably follows when they are not chosen to parent the child with whom they had been linked.

## Key findings

### Recruitment

- Over 95 per cent of the agencies responding to the survey did not have an adequate pool of adopters to offer a considerable choice of families for BME children, children with disabilities or children with special health needs. Ninety per cent of the agencies reported not having an adequate pool of adopters for older children. In contrast, 24 per cent reported a considerable choice of prospective adopters for sibling groups.
- Although it is difficult to find adoptive families for BME children, or those with disabilities or special health needs, about a quarter of the agencies said that they never specifically recruited adopters for these groups of children.

### Variation in practice in preparation and assessment of prospective adopters

Initial analysis of the total number of agencies that used any particular tools or approaches for adopter preparation and assessment showed a significant difference between the proportion of local authorities (35%; 20 of 57) and the proportion of voluntary agencies (65%; 11 of 17) that did so (p = 0.048 Fisher's exact test). However, an analysis of the free-text responses showed that only a minority of the tools and approaches mentioned seemed to stand out from routine practice. Of the initial 31 agencies that responded, only 15 described an approach that would qualify as more "innovative". If we take into account only these agencies, eight of the 57 local authorities (14%) fall into his category as do four of 17 voluntary adoption agencies (24%). This difference is not significant.

We identified four themes in this area of work that could potentially be important in linking and matching. Three of these themes relate to assessment and one to preparation:

- **Adult attachment**: Similar to the approach noted in the work with children, the use of adult attachment theory in relation to adopters is increasingly being used by adoption agencies. Fourteen per cent of agencies indicated the use of, or an interest in, the AAI or ASI.

- **Concurrency planning**: Although 16 per cent of agencies said they used a form of concurrency planning, only one agency elaborated on this in this section of the survey. This approach requires a rather specific form of preparation and assessment, as each carer needs to be prepared to be the foster carer as well as the prospective adopter of the same child or sibling group.

- **Assessment by two workers**: Although just one agency described this approach, it saw this as resulting in a more thorough assessment than would otherwise be the case.

- **Involvement of experienced adopters**: A recent study by Selwyn and Misca (2006) showed that a mentoring scheme was one of the services desired by prospective adopters. Although several agencies used experienced adopters to some extent in the preparation and adoption process of prospective adopters, only two agencies mentioned such a specific linking system. This system was used in particular for prospective adopters with similar characteristics, e.g. same-sex couples or people wanting to adopt sibling groups.

## After approval

- Most voluntary agencies (60%) referred adopters to the Adoption Register straight away, whereas most local authorities (85%) referred adopters three months after approval.

- In 60 per cent (nine of 15) of the voluntary agencies, adopters were free to embark on their own search for a child, if they wished, immediately after approval, compared to only 20 per cent (eight of 39) of local authorities. For local authorities, the more usual timescale was that adopters could look more widely three months after approval, or it was said to depend on the individual case.

- When a potential link had been made for adopters, 70 per cent of agencies routinely informed their adopters about each link, but 30 per cent did not.

# 6 Family finding

This chapter focuses on how agencies go about finding a family for a child. As case-holding responsibility for children lies only with local authorities, the findings in this chapter will sum up the responses from the 62 local authorities that completed this part of the questionnaire.

## Profiling children

A number of children may be matched with families fairly swiftly within an agency's own resources. However, for other children, depending on their needs, it will be necessary to search further afield. In such circumstances, a child's profile may play an important role in the family-finding process. In some cases the profile is very basic – only a written profile to fit on a flyer – but in others, the profile can be more comprehensive, using several photographs or a DVD that features the child. The greater the difficulty in finding a family, the more extensive the search will be.

All agencies used a written account of the child and in 98 per cent they also used a photograph to profile children. Seventy-two per cent have also used videos or DVDs for some children, and a few mentioned using the child's artwork or written views.

In the majority of agencies (90%), the child's profile was developed with input from several people, in order to get a complete picture of the child's needs and characteristics. In most cases, the child's social worker (93%) and foster carers (83%) were involved, sometimes also using input from the child (53%). Obviously, children's contributions will depend on their age. In a quarter of agencies, an internal marketing officer was used and another quarter mentioned the help of a specialist adoption worker or family finder. Hardly any agencies (only three) routinely used an external specialist, but 25 per cent of the agencies said they would occasionally hire an external company to assist in the development of profiles for children.

The child's social worker had the main responsibility for developing the child's profile in only 21 per cent of agencies. Workers specialising in adoption, permanence or family placement took responsibility for this task in 70 per cent of agencies, although input from the child's social worker and foster carer was integral to this process in almost all agencies (93% and 80% respectively). The duty was shared between the child's social worker and a specialist in seven per cent of agencies, and two per cent of respondents indicated that a recruitment officer developed profiles for children.

The number of hours spent on preparing a child's profile will depend on the child's needs and the availability of suitable adopters within the agency's direct resources. Looking at the last profile they had prepared, it took agencies on average five hours to develop a child's profile when this was not a particularly complex case (N = 42, SD = 4.5, range = 1–5). Seven agencies gave the number of hours for a complex case, with an average of 8.7 (SD = 5.2, range = 2–15).

*Figure 6.1*
**How many hours did it take agencies to prepare a child's profile?**

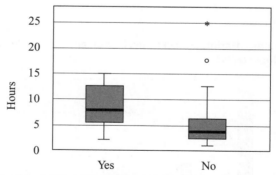

*Was this child's profile particularly complex to prepare?*

*Note: The symbols appearing above the bar on the right hand side indicate "outlying" values. In this case, two responses were numerically distant from the majority of responses.*

Of course, the more elaborate the profile, the more time it will take to prepare. For example, a profile prepared for adopter information events might comprise five minutes or so of video footage of the child at play, possibly in different contexts, along with an interview or commentary provided by the child's foster carer. The video may be complemented by more or less elaborate posters – often created by the child during direct work sessions. Clearly, such a profile will take substantially longer to put together than a few lines of text and a photograph.

## Family finding

Having assessed a child as needing an adoptive placement and established the child's needs and other characteristics that should be matched in the new family, the focus of the work moves to identifying families which might be able to meet a child's needs. In 80 per cent of local authorities, an adoption or family placement worker had the main responsibility for family finding. In other agencies, responsibility for family finding was mostly shared by more than one worker (often the child's social worker and an adoption worker).

The person responsible for family finding did not always meet with the

*Figure 6.2*
**Does the family-finding worker meet with or talk to the child when family finding starts?**

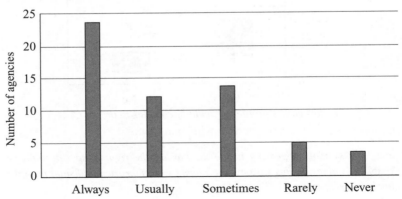

child she or he was finding a family for, as is shown in Figure 6.2. Fourteen per cent rarely or never met the child. However, in all agencies the family finder met with or talked to the child's social worker, and with the foster carers in 88 per cent of the agencies.

Not surprisingly, when a family which had been approved within the agency might be able to meet the child's needs, most agencies (82%) would first pursue the potential of that family before embarking on a wider search. The research has highlighted a number of issues in terms of how agencies approach family finding and their willingness to procure inter-agency placements; these are discussed further in Chapter 7.

We were interested in exploring how agencies dealt with situations where no suitable link could be found for a child. What were their strategies to reduce delays when family finding did not prove fruitful?

It is often suggested that, in the past, agencies have sometimes spent too long looking for the "ideal" family, which has led to delays for children. We were therefore keen to learn if and when agencies would relax the matching criteria if no links had been found for a child. In this survey, 31 per cent said that they would relax, or rather review, the matching criteria three months after the child was approved for adoption (i.e. an adoption recommendation was made) if no family had been found; a further 10 per cent would do so between three and six months after recommendation; and 39 per cent would wait between six to nine months. Just two agencies (4%) would wait longer than this, but eight agencies (16%) said they would never relax the matching criteria.

We also asked agencies at what point they would reconsider whether adoption was the appropriate plan, if no suitable link was found for a child. The majority of agencies (67%) said they would reconsider the plan six to nine months after the adoption recommendation. A minority of agencies (11%) would review the plan before six months and 20 per cent said they would leave it longer than nine months before reconsidering. Just one agency (2%) said they would never do so. The variation in approach is illustrated by the following comments:

> *If we have not identified a family **within six months** of active family finding then the plan should be reconsidered.* [Emphasis added] Shire county

*If the plan is for adoption and we have not been able to find a family,
e.g. after a couple of years, we may seek to change the plan.*
[Emphasis added] Unitary authority

## Linking children and families

We use the term "linking" here to refer to the process of identifying
families who may be able to meet a child's needs. In sum, this process is
about clarifying the needs of the child and identifying the sorts of
characteristics to be looked for in a family in order to meet those needs.
The Child's Permanence Report (CPR) (formerly Form E) is, in part,
intended to provide a clear description of the child's needs. In a similar
vein, the Prospective Adopter's Report (PAR) (formerly Form F) highlights the skills, capacities and characteristics that a family can offer. In
principle, these forms should allow for a comparison of children's needs
and families' strengths to produce a shortlist of families which may be
suitable.

Depending on the needs of specific children, the task of finding a
family which can meet those needs may be more or less demanding. For
some children, agencies will have a sufficient pool of approved adopters
able to offer all of the characteristics specified as being necessary for
the child. However, as discussed in Chapter 5, respondents frequently
reported difficulties in recruiting adoptive families for children with
particular needs. For some children, there may a particular requirement
that cannot be met within the agency's own resources and a wider search
will be needed.

It will, of course, also depend on the circumstances of the agency as
to whether they are in a position to recruit sufficient adopters with the
characteristics required. This is particularly the case in relation to matching children with black and minority ethnic (BME) backgrounds.
Figure 6.3 illustrates the sequence and the options available to agencies to
find appropriate families.

As outlined in Figure 6.3 opposite, agencies have at their disposal a
variety of mechanisms to facilitate the identification of potential links
between waiting children and available families. Figure 6.4 provides an
illustration of the extent to which each of these methods was reported to

*Figure 6.3*
**Steps followed in the family-finding process**

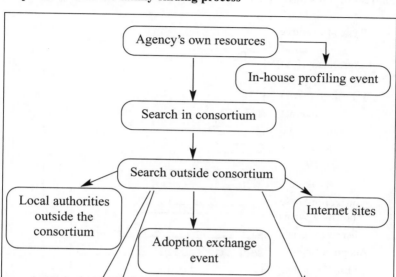

be used by the local authorities responding to this survey. Not all methods would have been equally available to all local authorities at the time of the survey; for example, newspapers for minority ethnic communities are not always national in their distribution. Internet websites were only just becoming nationally available at the time of writing but are included for the sake of completeness.

For each method listed, agencies were asked to indicate whether this resource accounted for "all, most, some, or a few" of the links made in the

*Figure 6.4*
**Sources of links in the past three years**

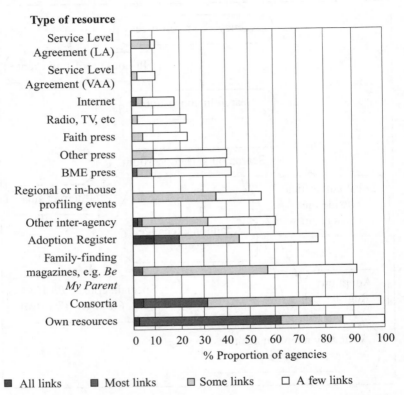

LA = local authority; VAA = voluntary adoption agency; BME = black and minority ethnic

past three years. As can be seen, all agencies made use of their own resources. For the majority of agencies (60%), their own resources were sufficient in most cases, but relatively few – only three per cent – had been able to place *all* of the children for whom they were responsible without recourse to other methods of finding links. This means that a sizeable minority of agencies (37%) were at least moderately reliant on other resources.

The figure also shows that inter-agency placements through consortia activities, featuring children in magazines such as *Be My Parent* or *Children Who Wait*,[11] and referral of children to the Adoption Register were used by a substantial proportion of agencies (98%, 92% and 75% of agencies respectively), although the proportions of links made through these channels varied. Placements secured through "other inter-agency" arrangements would probably include those resulting from periodic mailings between agencies of children's details in the hope that a child's profile might match the characteristics of a family approved by another agency. Just over half of the agencies reported such links being made, although they rarely accounted for the majority of links made by any one agency.

Less often used were more general media resources such as radio, TV and the news media, although several agencies did use these methods with some success. Service Level Agreements (see glossary in Appendix B) with either voluntary agencies or other local authorities were relatively rarely used and only ever accounted for a minority of links secured (see also Deloitte, 2006).

As many as half of the agencies had secured some links through regional adoption events or in-house profiling events. This sort of approach has been used by certain agencies for some time, but the methods are relatively new in mainstream UK adoption practice, although their use is growing fast. Regional events are usually organised by a consortium of adoption agencies and sometimes by the Adoption Register. They vary in the precise way they are organised but, briefly, the method involves bringing professionals, and sometimes adopters, together from a variety of agencies to feature children and families who are waiting for a match. In-house profiling events take a different stance, seeking to present a fuller picture of a child, using a variety of media, to a gathering

---

[11]   These are periodic magazines featuring photographs and written profiles of children who need an adoptive family. They are produced by BAAF and Adoption UK respectively and circulated to approved adopters and adoption professionals.

of prospective adoptive families who have been, or are in the process of being, approved by the agency (Cousins, 2003 and 2005). Broad indicators are given about the sort of family that is sought and families are then encouraged to contact the social worker about any child whom they think they might be able to parent. This adopter-led approach builds on the paper-based featuring of children's profiles in the specialist magazines but allows for more of the "whole child" to be seen. The method demands substantial amounts of professional time and resources in building the profiles, organising the event and following up on enquiries. However, its proponents are agreed that it is a means of securing adoptive placements for children who are "hard to place", i.e. those whose characteristics on paper might appear never to match with what a family can provide.

Featuring children on the internet provided some links for around 17 per cent of agencies. Until recently, the use of the internet to feature children has been a highly contentious issue, and understandably so, given the need for confidentiality and concerns about who may be able to access information (BAAF, 2005a–c). However, things are moving rapidly on this front and in a recent survey Barnett and Moroney (2004) identified 15 internet websites that profiled children, and Freundlich and colleagues (2007) reviewed the way these resources are used across the US, Canada and Russian Federation. The use of the internet has not been a central focus of this part of the research but we have identified two major internet services that have been active in this field up to now. One is London Kids, a site that allows public access but uses photographs of models, pseudonyms and very general or altered descriptions to maintain confidentiality. London Kids is operated by a consortium of 18 London boroughs (www.londonkids.org.uk). The other internet service is operated by Adoption 22, a consortium of 22 local authorities in the north-west of England that works in association with seven voluntary adoption agencies. Their website (www.lookafterme.co.uk) went live in April 2006 (Dyer, 2002). This internet resource differs from that of London Kids in two ways. First, the database includes waiting children and approved families from all member agencies and second, it is a closed system – it can be accessed only by nominated professionals within any member agency. More recently, BAAF's own internet resource for family finding and linking (www.bemyparent.org.uk) has also gone live on the web

(O'Reilly, 2007). It might be expected that this form of finding links will account for an increasing proportion of links in the future.

It can be seen, then, that adoption agencies are often imaginative and inventive in their search for ways of locating families whose characteristics will match the needs of the children they need to place.

In considering the mechanics of each of the approaches listed above, it is clear that there are four major approaches to linking. The first is where professionals (or, in the case of the Adoption Register, a computer system with some oversight by trained administrators and professionals) compare written or coded information about a child to similar information about a family and make judgements about the degree of compatibility between the two. Of course, potential links which may be initiated in this way will subsequently be explored in much more detail by the respective workers.

The second is where potential links are available in-house. In these cases, workers will immediately be aware of the families on their books, the qualities they have to offer, and areas in which they may need support in order to parent a particular child. In this situation, the links are professionally led but differ from those described previously, in that individual workers within the same agency are likely to know each other and can be pro-active in advocating for the families they have been working with.

In the third approach, information about the child is simply presented through words, pictures and sometimes videos (or DVDs) to the community of approved adopters. These families, or those working with them, are then invited to come forward and discuss whether what they have to offer might be right for the child. This method and the final one might properly be described as "adopter led".

The final approach is where the information about the child is featured outside the "adoption community" – i.e. in the public arena, as in the use of press, radio or TV. Here, individuals who may never have even considered adopting are asked to think about whether they might have what is needed for a particular child.

Most agencies responding to the survey used a combination of these methods to identify families, although a small number of local authorities use profiling events as a major tool for identifying suitable families for children they wish to place. The means by which links are identified for individual cases, as well as the practice of sharing children's profiles on videos or DVDs with adopters, will be examined in the second stage of the research.[12]

## Finance and inter-agency placements

One thorny area that must be discussed in relation to linking children and families for adoption is money. Unless agencies are able to place children within their own resources, or sometimes within their consortium resources, there will be a fee to be paid to the agency responsible for recruiting and preparing the adoptive family: the inter-agency fee. There was frequent reference throughout the questionnaire to this issue. The comment of one voluntary agency's manager responding to a question about obstacles to linking and matching summarises the view of many voluntary agencies:

> *Finance – local authorities are often unwilling to pay inter-agency fees to a voluntary organisation as a point of principle. It is often only after exhausting all other cheaper options.* Voluntary agency

The fee covering the costs of recruitment, assessment and preparation also covers that agency's support of the placement for the first year. There is a fixed scale of fees that is adjusted each year, but overall fees are greater for families recruited by voluntary agencies than by local authorities. The fees chargeable in 2005/06 by voluntary agencies were £19,408 for a single child placed by a local authority, as against £12,354 for placements purchased from another local authority. The placement of a sibling group incurs proportionately larger charges, while agencies based in London are able to charge an additional 10 per cent on all fees (BAAF, 2006). While inter-agency fees are payable for any inter-agency placement, some consortia operate on a no-fee or a reduced-fee basis. One consortium

---

[12] As mentioned in Chapter 2, a second stage of this study is underway. It will explore linking and matching on a case-by-case basis and will be published in due course by BAAF.

advised us that member agencies shared families for £8,000 – representing a considerable discount on the standard fee.

With this in mind, especially recognising the tremendous financial constraints on local authority services generally, it is not surprising that many local authorities first seek to place children with families recruited by their own agency (see the local authorities' comments below). However, there are both legislative and good practice incentives to place children within a reasonable time frame and these may militate against waiting for a suitable in-house placement to become available.

As we have seen, the local authorities responding to the questionnaire reported a wide variation in the number of children placed in the year 2005/06, from just five children in one agency to 96 children in another. This is not surprising since agencies vary in the size of population that they serve. However, there was also a substantial variation in the proportion of children who were placed within the agencies' own resources: one agency placed seven children but none were placed with their own adopters; another agency placed all but three of their 36 children in-house. On average (mean), agencies had paid an inter-agency fee in 40 per cent of their cases (range 0–100% and sd = 23.6). According to information obtained from finance officers elsewhere in the questionnaire, agencies had spent between £17,000 and £405,000 on inter-agency fees in the previous financial year; between £600 and £86,000 on consortium fees; and between £1,000 and £56,000 on Service Level Agreements (see glossary in Appendix B).

We asked respondents to indicate how readily their agencies were prepared to incur the costs of using the various search strategies. Fewer than 10 per cent of agencies reported reluctance to spend money, with the majority being equally divided between authorising these costs "very" and "fairly" readily. Only eight respondents recorded any restriction on the number of inter-agency placements that could be purchased. Reflecting on the previous year's experience, three agencies reported a potential link being refused because of budget restrictions. Some of the comments about these restrictions are presented in Figure 6.5 below. As these illustrate, the restrictions are not necessarily absolute.

Nonetheless, local authorities often proceed sequentially in their search for links, beginning with their own resources, proceeding to use

*Figure 6.5*
**Local authority comments on inter-agency budget restrictions**

> *A budget is set for inter-agency fees. This is reviewed regularly. If there is a predicted overspend, this is brought to the attention of the AD – with the hope of acquiring extra monies from elsewhere.*
>
> Metropolitan area

> *We have an annual budget, but we have a number of regular commitments. In realistic terms, this results in about seven new placements each year that we can plan for.*
>
> Metropolitan area

> *There are budget restraints. At least 60 per cent of children should be placed with agency adopters.*
>
> Metropolitan area

> *The adoption team are asked to explore all potential links internally or via the consortium before considering links that may incur inter-agency fees. Management are not usually prepared to consider fees until the child has been waiting about three to six months for a link – depending on the circumstances, e.g. sibling group, health issues, etc.*
>
> Shire county

families from their agency consortium if necessary, and only involving other agencies if they have no success with their own or local resources. Interestingly, a recent report (Selwyn *et al*, 2009) has shown that inter-agency fees are currently lower than placing a child for adoption internally when the full costs for local authorities are taken into account. However, since local authorities underestimate (or do not take into account) their own costs in finding an internal placement, inter-agency fees are perceived to be expensive.

Thinking about the varied use of inter-agency placement across agencies, we had asked a question towards the beginning of the questionnaire about particular issues for individual agencies in relation to linking and matching practice. The responses to this question, a sample of which are listed in Figure 6.6, are helpful in interpreting this variation.

*Figure 6.6*

**Issues regarding the recruitment of adopters in relation to inter-agency placements**

> *[This area] has numerous boroughs and councils all attempting to recruit from the same geographical area, plus a number of VAAs who also recruit from within* [the area].
>
> Metropolitan area

> *Have difficulty in placing our own BME children with our own BME adopters. Due to the geographical issues and there being tight community networks.*
>
> Metropolitan area

> *Small geographical area – high transient population – high drug and alcohol-related problems – large numbers of children removed through care proceedings. Small population to recruit adopters from.*
>
> Unitary authority

> *Small geographical area, plus many prospective adopters live in* [the city centre], *which makes external placement preferable.*
>
> Metropolitan area

> *Relatively small geographical area. Difficulty in recruiting BME adopters.*
>
> Unitary authority

> *BME adopters live in the same geographical areas that the children needing placements come from.*
>
> Shire county

> *The authority is geographically large and we vie with neighbouring outer-London boroughs to recruit. We also have VAAs in the area and a significant number of adopters want to adopt from overseas. The authority has pockets of deprivation and minority ethnic communities within an overall affluent white area.*
>
> Shire county

Essentially, there are three factors, aside from children's individual needs, which seem to lead to a far greater use of inter-agency placement by some agencies. These are, firstly, to do with the size or profile of the populations they serve: agencies operating in very small areas and/or very deprived areas are often unable to recruit families in sufficient numbers and may anyway wish to place outside the area to avoid complications with adoptive and birth families living too close to each other. Secondly, other agencies, although perhaps in larger and more mixed areas, report that they experience difficulty in recruiting families from particular minority communities for the children they need to place because these families tend to live in the same sectors of the area as do birth family members. A third issue is that of competition between agencies, when a number of agencies are trying to recruit adoptive parents from the same area.

## Deciding which families to proceed with

For some children, although not all, there will be a number of families which might, on paper, seem to meet their needs. Therefore, identifying families is only a starting point. The next step in the process is to try to shortlist those who can offer the most to a particular child. We wanted to explore with respondents how that process was managed within their agencies.

Agencies said they would, in general, pursue one (13 agencies), two (nine agencies) or more commonly three (25 agencies) links (potential

*Figure 6.7*
**The number of links that agencies will usually pursue at one time**

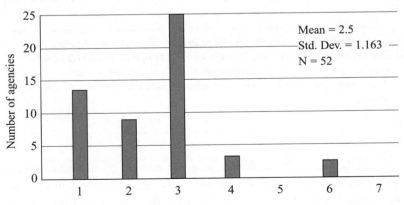

Mean = 2.5
Std. Dev. = 1.163
N = 52

*How many potential links will usually be pursued at any one time?*

families) at any one time, although a minority reported more (see Figure 6.7).

Of course, what can be gleaned from paper (the PAR, formerly Form F) will necessarily be limited and it is likely that further discussion will be needed in order to make informed choices, as observed by one of our respondents:

> [One needs] *a realistic understanding of the qualities and vulner-abilities of adopters – sometimes Form Fs are only as good as their authors – so some good matches may be lost – and some non-positive matches followed through on the basis of these.* Metropolitan area

From the responses to subsequent questions in this section, it seems that the majority of agencies followed up links primarily through discussions with the workers for the families involved, rather than with the families themselves. This was true for 96 per cent of the agencies, who said that workers would usually be contacted for all the families that had been shortlisted. In most agencies, family-finding workers would only some-times talk directly to the families involved, but in only a quarter of agencies did this happen routinely in the early stages of the linking process. Whether more than one family is made aware that they are being considered for a child is clearly, as we have seen, an area of some debate. One agency described their practice thus:

> *A permanency core group will identify families that may be able to meet children's needs using matching criteria tools. Shortlist of families will be visited and formal matching meeting held later if they are considered to be a good match for the child.* Shire county

However, as mentioned in Chapter 5, there is a tension between wishing to understand fully what a family can offer and the risk of repeatedly giving families false hope that they may soon have a child placed. The following comments illustrate the different positions and some of the reasons behind them:

> *The growing tendency to visit more than one family when considering a match is, in my view, unnecessary. A match should be made on*

*paper, the family visited and if not suitable [then the] second choice visited.* Voluntary agency

*Some local authorities visit a number of families, which leaves adopters anxiously waiting (sometimes for several weeks) for a decision.* Voluntary agency

*We have an agreement within [our consortium] that, except in exceptional circumstances, we will shortlist down to one family – and only that family would be visited. However, I feel strongly that there are exceptions to this, and so – particularly with older children or children with very specific needs – we would consider visiting two possible families, with the agreement of both agencies and with both families being aware of this.* Metropolitan area

Clearly, the task of fully understanding how the qualities of an adoptive family might meet a child's needs can be complex and time consuming in some cases. Respondents were asked to estimate how much time had been

*Figure 6.8*
**Number of hours spent talking with families or their workers to identify a link for children with complex and less complex needs**

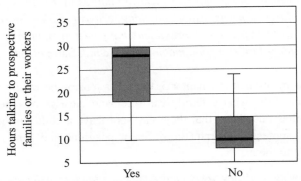

*Was the linking process for this child particularly complex?*

spent talking with families or their workers in the last linking process that they had experienced. Figure 6.8 illustrates the variation in responses to this question and, importantly, how this varied depending on the complexity of the child's needs. Caution is needed in interpreting the chart as numbers are fairly small in both groups (n = 17 for non-complex cases and just eight for complex cases). One agency recorded a figure of 163 hours, which is substantially higher than other estimates. This is not included in the chart because the number of hours indicated was so excessive compared to others that the chart would be difficult to interpret. Thus, agencies reporting on a complex case recorded an average of 24 hours (range 10–35 and sd = 9.6), while those reporting a less complex case recorded an average of 11 hours (range 5–24 and sd = 5.2).

## Key findings

- Almost all agencies produced profiles for at least some of the children they wanted to place for adoption. Profiles were predominantly the responsibility of the adoption or family-finding team and were usually developed in-house: just a quarter of agencies reported sometimes using external companies in this process.
- The time taken to prepare profiles is likely to depend on the complexity of the child's needs, where the profile is to be featured and how well the worker knows the case. Agencies reported between one and 25 hours, with an average of five hours, spent on this task.
- Agencies varied in terms of if, or when, they would reconsider the matching criteria if no match had been found: 41 per cent would review three to six months after approval and 39 per cent after six to nine months, while others were prepared to wait longer. However, 16 per cent said they would never relax the matching criteria.
- There was similar variation in relation to the point at which agencies would reconsider whether adoption was the appropriate plan if no suitable link was found for a child. The majority (67%) said they would reconsider the plan six to nine months after the adoption recommendation. A minority of agencies (11%) would review the plan before six months and 20 per cent said they would leave it longer than

nine months before reconsidering. Just one agency (2%) said they would never do so.

- Agencies used a wide variety of family-finding methods to identify potential links for children, although the proportion of links made through each mechanism varied. Agencies' own resources, their consortium arrangements, the family-finding press and the Adoption Register were most frequently used. Service Level Agreements were used relatively rarely.

- Half of the agencies had secured some links through regional exchange events or in-house profiling events. Featuring children on the internet provided some links for 17 per cent of the agencies.

- Agencies varied in their ability to place children within their own resources. On average, agencies paid an inter-agency fee for 40 per cent of placements made. About 10 per cent of agencies reported a reluctance to pay for inter-agency placements, and three agencies stated that a link had been refused because of budget restrictions.

- Local authorities often proceed sequentially in their search for links, beginning with their own resources, proceeding to use families from their agency consortium if necessary and only involving voluntary agencies if they have no success with their own or local resources.

- We identified three factors that seemed relevant to the variation in the use of inter-agency placements across local authorities. These were:

  - Agencies operating in small or deprived areas find it hard to recruit local families who are able to adopt and, for various reasons, they may wish to place out of area anyway.

  - Some agencies have very small minority ethnic populations but do need to place children of minority heritage, whilst others avoid placing BME children with minority communities in their authority because the families often live in the same sector as the children's birth families.

  - In some areas, there is significant competition between adoption agencies to recruit from a finite pool of potential adoptive families.

- In most agencies, decisions about which families to proceed with were informed, in the early stages, by discussion with workers for the families rather than with the families themselves. This process could be time consuming and agencies estimated that such discussions absorbed between five and 35 hours for the last child linked, with an average of 24 hours for complex cases and an average of 11 for a less complex case.

- Agencies said they would in general pursue one (13 agencies), two (nine agencies) or more commonly three (25 agencies) links at any one time, although a minority reported more. There were differing views about the appropriateness of approaching more than one family at a time about a particular child.

# 7 Key factors in making a match

Because so little has been written about matching, we felt that the most useful way of exploring the experiences of respondents was to ask fairly open questions to get at the fundamental issues in this sphere of practice. To this end, we asked:

- What are the key factors in making a good match, in your experience?
- What are the key factors that should preclude a match, in your experience?
- What do you think are the biggest barriers to linking and matching children to prospective adopters?
- Are there any other issues in relation to linking and matching that have not been mentioned elsewhere in this questionnaire?

The free-text responses to these questions were entered into a qualitative analysis package and coded for themes. About four in five of the agencies that responded to this section of our questionnaire (58 of 74) reported that their agency held the responsibility for making decisions about the families with which children should be placed.

## Key factors in matching

In this section, we concentrate on those factors that respondents mentioned as "key to a good match" and those that "should preclude a match". In many ways, the factors that were thought to preclude a match were the flipside of those raised in relation to making a good match. However, issues that are felt to have a positive influence on matching are not necessarily the opposite of those that preclude a match.

Although there was substantial variation, and much overlap, in the responses to these questions, we identified several distinct themes. We have grouped these themes in such a way that we look first at factors that primarily concern the way services operate: we have named these "practice, process and organisational factors". Our second theme is related to the characteristics of adoptive families: in this context, we focus on families' circumstances and experiences. The third group of factors relates to adopters' attitudes and understanding of adoption issues and their own emotional preparedness for adoption. There were two additional factors – "chemistry" and children's views, which we deal with at the end of this section.

In each of these sub-sections, we begin by presenting a graphic illustration of the main factors mentioned, with some indication of the frequency with which each was mentioned and in what context. The accompanying text elaborates on these themes and provides illustrations of the sorts of comments made and views expressed by respondents.

## Factors related to practice, process and organisation

Figure 7.1 lists ten factors that can be seen as a function of the way that practice is undertaken and the way individual practitioners and agencies work together.

At the top of this list, by a long margin, is the need for accurate information about the child on which to base family-finding plans and matching. Respondents felt strongly that the information provided should be clear, accurate and up to date. A few respondents also thought there should be a hierarchy of the child's needs to facilitate matching.

*Current and clear assessment of the child (including a report from the current carer); a social worker who is knowledgeable about the child and clear about what they are looking for in a placement; well written and full reports which ensure that the adopters feel confident about the material they are dealing with.* Voluntary agency

*List those needs that must be met, followed by a second list of those most desirable.* Unitary authority

It follows logically from this that respondents thought assessments needed to be adequate; this was often mentioned at the same time as emphasising the importance of good preparation for both children and adopters. Apart from good preparation, respondents also considered that recognition of and provision for adoption support needs were important.

*Figure 7.1*
**Key factors in matching: practice, process and organisation**

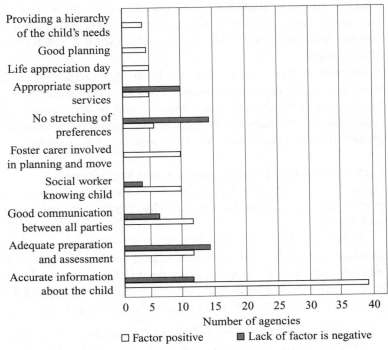

*Social workers who know the children and are committed to ensuring that they receive all the appropriate specialist services (e.g. health, education, therapy). Thorough preparation and life story work undertaken with children. This includes direct work, not just compiling a life story book. Adoptive parents who have been thoroughly prepared for the task, have a robust support network and an ability to advocate on behalf of children.* Voluntary agency

A number of agencies (13) mentioned the extent to which the child's social worker was familiar with the child's case. In many cases this was framed, as in the quotation above, to imply that a social worker's familiarity with the case would enhance the likelihood of a good match. Three agencies suggested that multiple changes of social workers could preclude a match.

Several respondents also stressed that agencies have a responsibility not to rush the matching process, to explore doubts and uncertainties as they arose, to allow time for a family to reflect without feeling pressured, and to match with as little "stretching" as possible. Encouraging families to consider children outside their preferred age range was frequently mentioned as a way of stretching preferences.

[Good match] *Time for reflection during the matching period. No pressure on a family to consider a match they are uncomfortable with.* Voluntary agency

[Preclude a match] *If carers are stretching their assessed capacity, e.g. age of the child.* London borough

[Preclude a match] *Minimising of the child's needs to try to force a fit.* Shire county

Other factors, on a practice level, that were considered important to making a good match were: involving the foster carer in providing information about the child and helping the child move on; considering the views of the birth family; and, although not strictly a part of the matching process, having a Life Appreciation Day[13] once a match had been approved.

Within this broad theme, there were also factors to do with the culture of the organisation (the adoption agency). People wrote about: the importance of management support; common values and standards; working together (especially having positive working relationships between children's social workers and family-finding workers, and foster carers working positively towards the move); being clear about planning

---

[13]  A Life Appreciation Day is held to give prospective adopters the chance to meet significant people in the child's life (e.g. teachers, nurses, previous carers) in order to exchange information and understand more of the child's history.

and achieving consensus; and communication between professionals, local authorities and voluntary agencies. Communication was also mentioned in relation to prospective adopters: they should be able to work with the agencies and be open with them.

*If there is not a respectful, professional relationship between the two agencies, it is very difficult to support a placement, so this is a danger sign!* Voluntary agency

*In inter-agency placements the key is to have common values and standards and good, well-established working arrangements – as with the consortium.* Unitary authority

### Factors related to adopters' characteristics and circumstances

*Figure 7.2*
**Key factors in matching: adopters' characteristics**

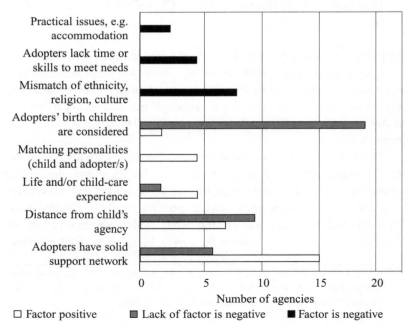

□ Factor positive     ▨ Lack of factor is negative     ■ Factor is negative

A second group of factors reflected the practical attributes and circumstances of families; these are shown in Figure 7.2. Some felt it important that the lifestyle, personalities and interests of family members should match the child's personality and interests. Several respondents said that a mismatch between the adopters' and the child's ethnicity, religion or culture could preclude a match.

*The family needs to have awareness of the child's heritage and a genuine willingness to develop their knowledge of and contacts with that community, and to promote the child in developing a positive sense of his/her identity.* Voluntary agency

*We would be wary of a match which did not meet the child's ethnic or cultural profile – there would be occasions where this would preclude the match.* Metropolitan area

[Good match] *Congruency between the adopters' lifestyle and parenting style with the child's interests and personality.* Voluntary agency

Many respondents mentioned the importance of the views and ages of families' birth children. In fact, where birth children's needs in a proposed placement might conflict with those of the child, this was seen by many agencies as a factor that should preclude a match.

*Other children in the family – will the adopted child fill their emotional and physical space?* London borough

Respondents also often noted the importance of families' support networks. Geographical distance was considered key by some, but there were interesting differences in what respondents meant by this. Where some respondents said that geography should be appropriate – meaning the adoptive family should not live too close to the birth family, others interpreted geographical distance as meaning that the adoptive family should not live too far from the adoption agency as it would complicate placement support.

Some respondents considered the life experience or child-care experience of prospective adopters to be an important factor in matching.

Some also noted factors relating to adopters lacking the time or skills to meet the child's particular needs. Finally, some said that practical issues such as accommodation could preclude a match, although the converse was not mentioned as a factor that would make a good match.

## Factors related to adopters' attitudes and understanding

*Figure 7.3*
**Key factors in matching: adopters' attitudes and understanding**

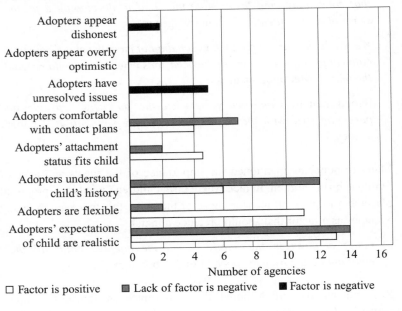

A third group of factors related to adopters' personal attributes (shown in Figure 7.3) for example, their expectations of the adoptive placement. Respondents thought this factor was both key in making a good match and that it should also preclude a match when adopters were expecting far too much from a child. One respondent formulated it as: 'adopters expecting the child to fulfil their needs instead of them meeting the child's needs'. In relation to this, one of the obstacles mentioned was where adopters (or social workers) were overly optimistic about a placement and did not recognise any possible problems. Respondents felt quite strongly about the importance of adopters understanding the child's history and the needs that history brings with it. In addition, adopters needed to be able to empathise with the child's birth family.

[Preclude a match] *Lack of appreciation and understanding of child's needs – how what has happened to them will come out in the placement.* London borough

Apart from understanding the realities of adoption and the child, it was emphasised that adoptive parents needed to show flexibility. Although few respondents mentioned inflexibility as a factor that should preclude the match, many saw flexibility as a key factor to good matching.

*Adopters who show a readiness to adapt and who can be flexible.* Voluntary agency

Contact was mentioned by several respondents, although not always in the same context. Where contact was noted as a key factor to a good match, the respondents thought that the adoptive family needed to be comfortable with the contact arrangements. However, where contact was mentioned as a factor that could preclude a match, there was a notable difference in opinion. Two voluntary agencies thought 'the level of contact shouldn't be too high, as adopters will not be able to cope with that', but, in contrast, five local authorities thought 'adopters should be open to the contact arrangements as they are'. These two views may reflect the different stance adopted by the family's agency or worker and that of the child's.

*Level of contact could be disruptive to the placement.* Voluntary agency

[Preclude a match] *Adopters unwilling to accept contact deemed to be in the child's best interest.* Unitary authority

Some knowledge of the attachment style or status of both adoptive parent and child was a factor of importance to some, whilst others felt that when adopters had unresolved issues (mostly about infertility), this should preclude a match.

[Good match] *Secure attachment patterns in adopters and child; warmth and empathy in adopters.* Shire county

Finally, the quality of the assessment of adopters was noted as crucial, so that a realistic understanding of their qualities and vulnerabilities could be reached. As we noted earlier, one respondent commented that, 'Form Fs are only as good as their authors – so some good matches may be lost – and some non-positive matches followed through on the basis of these'.

## Additional factors in matching: "chemistry" and children's views

There were two factors that did not fit into any of the groups described so far. The first was about "emotional connectedness with a particular child" or "chemistry". Although it was only mentioned twice, and respondents did not elaborate on their answers, we feel it should be included here. The importance of "chemistry" between adoptive parent and child was mentioned by Festinger (1990) in her discussion of adoption disruption, and more recently by Sinclair and Wilson (2003) in relation to successful foster placements. Positive chemistry is, of course, something that is almost impossible to plan for, but Sinclair and Wilson certainly argue that (particularly for older children) it is something that should be respected when it occurs. It is likely that the formation of an emotional connection, at least on the part of adoptive families, might be facilitated by the more recent developments in adopter-led linking methods (discussed earlier), although it is also possible that such a bond might blind potential adopters to issues they might not be able to manage in the longer term. At this point, there has been little research on this approach to linking and it is something that is being explored in the second stage of this study.

The second factor that stood apart from the others was the importance of the child's views on the proposed placement, as described by the following respondent:

*I also think key issues for matching are about looking at the expectations of the child as well as the adopter(s) . . . We have learned – too late – that two children had a very definite picture in mind of what their adoptive family looked like, and their prospective adopters*

*did not match this at all . . . If, during introductions, the child was not able to relate and build up the beginnings of a relationship, or if there was tension with one of the adopters or with their children, we would seriously consider halting the process.* Metropolitan area

Children's views about proposed placements were a second major factor identified by Sinclair and Wilson (2003), and the importance of children's understanding and wishes has been highlighted by many other authors (see, e.g. Dance and Rushton, 2005), while Lord (2008) cites work reporting that children's views are important when choosing a family to adopt a child. It is perhaps somewhat surprising that only seven respondents mentioned hearing the child's views, taking it as a key factor to preclude a match when a child did not want to be adopted or was opposed to the placement (see also Selwyn *et al*, 2008). However, it is possible that many respondents thought of very young children when responding to these questions and so did not mention this particular factor.

## Barriers to matching and other issues

The factors that respondents identified as barriers to matching again separated into different categories. One of the major themes emerging from this section of the analysis concerned financial issues – in particular, the cost and/or reluctance to pay the fees for inter-agency placements, especially with voluntary adoption agencies. This issue has been discussed in some detail elsewhere in the report and will not be repeated here. A second major theme involved social work issues, particularly the attitudes of some children's social workers.

Other themes touched on the perennial dilemmas in adoption practice, highlighted by Rushton in 2000: contact with the birth family, matching on ethnicity, and issues around sibling placement were all mentioned. Figures 7.5 to 7.7 present a few comments on each of these areas to illustrate the variety of opinions given.

Finally, a small number of agencies introduced other issues here: the situation of same-sex couples, birth parent involvement in adoption plans and variation in adoption practice between agencies (see Figure 7.8).

*Figure 7.4*
**Issues concerning social work**

> Social workers' own values and preconceptions about adopters from reading Form F and rejecting them before seeing them. Form Fs are not always written in a way that "sells" a family.
>
> Shire county

> Social workers who won't even agree to discuss a child with adopters if they are not quite what they initially wanted.
>
> Unitary authority

> Inexperienced social workers who have not had sufficient training in care planning and matching.
>
> Shire county

> Judgemental social workers with preconceived ideas of the "ideal" family.
>
> Voluntary agency

> Social workers who do not know the child or who are emotionally over-involved with them.
>
> Voluntary agency

*Figure 7.5*
**Issues concerning contact**

> Some adoption agencies still approve prospective adopters who are not open to contact. We do not approve prospective adopters who are categorical that they would never manage contact, as we feel this does not demonstrate the necessary openness to responding to a child's changing needs in relation to contact over the years.
>
> Unitary authority

> Some contact plans (especially if defined by court).
>
> Shire county

> Excessive contact arrangements.
>
> Voluntary agency

*Figure 7.6*
**Issues concerning ethnicity**

> *How to assess which of a child's competing needs take priority, given the complex backgrounds, particularly ethnic and religious backgrounds, which many of our children have.*
> Unitary authority

> *Trying to place children in a racial and cultural match is sometimes difficult.*
> Unitary authority

*Figure 7.7*
**Issues concerning siblings**

> *Sometimes siblings cannot be placed together in adoptive placements so needs have to be weighed up. For example, if we couldn't find an adoptive family within a child-centred timescale but we could find foster carers, etc. How long before we would do this depends on the issue as it relates to the child.*
> Shire county

> *Preparation of siblings of children moving to adoptive families is also a very important part of this work* [and] *work with other siblings in family is crucial.*
> Shire county

> *Keeping siblings together ONLY if this is a result of a full assessment.* [Original emphasis]
> Unitary authority

*Figure 7.8*
**Other issues**

> *Over a quarter of our prospective adopters are same-sex couples. We would want to highlight the positive contribution that same-sex adopters can make in widening the pool of prospective adopters. We do encounter reluctance on behalf of some agencies to use same-sex adopters.*
>
> Unitary authority

> *People must keep the bigger picture at the forefront of their minds when considering families, in my experience. People will always plump for two-parent households over single applicants, for example.*
>
> London borough

> *Unfortunately, usually due to the situation in proceedings, we do not draw on the birth parents' views enough – and again this is something I believe we should be developing.*
>
> Metropolitan area

> *Enormous variations in practice between agencies can sometimes make inter-agency placements very difficult and time consuming, particularly where we are providing the adoptive family.*
>
> Shire county

## Summary

This chapter has endeavoured to communicate the knowledge and understanding of a group of experienced professionals working in adoption. Respondents were presented with broad, open questions and invited to answer in terms of their own experience and priorities. The material makes it clear that the process of matching children and families relies on a multiplicity of factors coming together: some within, and some outside, the control of any particular agency or individual.

We have seen that the way in which practice is undertaken and services are organised is thought by respondents to be critical to making a good match. There were also practical considerations about families' circumstances and a need to take into account adopters' attitudes, levels of understanding and ability to empathise.

There was a clear call for the information available in the Child's Permanence Report (CPR) to be accurate and up to date, which is, of course, a common refrain (see e.g. Selwyn *et al*, 2008). This survey was conducted shortly after the implementation of the Adoption and Children Act 2002 and the accompanying regulations, which tightened up procedures for adoption, so it remains to be seen whether these new arrangements will result, in time, in more frequent updating or better quality control of the information provided in the CPR.

Of particular note was the apparent centrality of the role of the children's social worker, not only in terms of their completion of the CPR, but also in their holding knowledge of the children's history, and understanding their needs in placement. Two issues emerged in relation to this. One was the all-too-frequent situation whereby children experience multiple changes of worker. Recruitment and retention of staff in children's services has long been acknowledged as an issue that requires addressing, and indeed this is currently the focus of the Children's Workforce Development Council (CWDC) (www.cwdcouncil.org.uk) and the Social Work Task Force. However, experience tells us that change is sometimes built into the process in the way in which services are organised and it frequently happens also as a result of reorganisation of services. These concerns require solutions at the broader strategic management level. The second issue emerged as a barrier to matching – where several respondents highlighted prejudices or preconceptions on the part of some children's social workers. This might be somewhat ameliorated with further training. Alternatively, it might be useful to reconsider the role of the children's worker as the final decision maker on which adoptive family to choose.

Another major theme was communication within agencies, between agencies and with adoptive families. Respondents highlighted, in particular, variation in practice between agencies as a potential difficulty in inter-agency placements.

Responses to this section of the questionnaire not only drew attention to the ongoing dilemmas in adoption work that concern the placement of siblings, birth family contact and ethnicity, but also introduced the need to think more openly about single adopters and same-sex couples.

## Key findings

- Responses to the open questions on factors making for a good match or that should preclude a match fell largely into three broad categories, with two additional elements:
  - service factors related to social work practice, the adoption process and the way the agency operates as an organisation;
  - factors relating to adopters' circumstances, including where they live, their interests, their support networks and their other children;
  - factors relating to adopters' attitudes and experience, particularly their ability to understand the impact of children's earlier experiences, their own attachment status or style, comfort with contact plans and being "realistic";
  - emotional connectedness or "chemistry" and the importance of children's views were also mentioned by a minority.
- The importance of the role of the children's social worker came across in terms of both continuity and knowledge of the child, in the preparation of the children's paperwork and in their controlling role in terms of choosing a family.
- An exploration of respondents' thoughts about barriers to matching reaffirmed an ongoing difficulty in how to make judgements and formulate plans about:
  - matching for children of black or minority ethnic backgrounds;
  - placement of sibling groups;
  - contact with birth families.
- Further barriers included the variation in practice across agencies, children's social workers' preconceived ideas about the "ideal" family for the child, and workers' preconceptions about the suitability of families with non-traditional structures.
- Concerns about agencies' willingness to incur inter-agency fees were also revisited in this context.

# 8  Priorities and issues in matching

In the previous chapter, we explored responses to a series of open questions about matching, which gave respondents the opportunity to indicate their own priorities and provide some context for their answers. In this chapter, we relay information obtained through two sets of closed questions that aimed to unpick, more systematically, the degree of importance that professionals attach to specific areas of need when thinking about matching.

First, we asked respondents to rate the relative importance, in their view, of a variety of factors that are relevant to the matching process. The answer options were "essential", "desirable", "of a lower priority" or "not important". The frequency of responses for each factor examined is illustrated in Figure 8.1.

Quite properly, the overwhelming emphasis in matching appears to be on the child's characteristics. Meeting children's behavioural, attachment and health or disability needs was almost universally considered "essential". Taking into consideration their wishes, temperaments, appearance and talents was, however, thought less critical by some respondents. (Matching around children's temperaments, wishes, appearance and talents were marked as essential by 55%, 41%, 36% and 24% of respondents respectively.)

Adopters' parenting styles were seen as crucial by about 80 per cent of respondents and adopters' wishes were seen as essential to match by about two-thirds. Meeting the wishes of birth families or foster carers was rarely seen as essential, although this was quite frequently described as desirable.

Considerations in relation to contact plans, ethnicity and geography (the physical location of the placement in relation to the child's area of origin) were thought to be essential by one-half to two-thirds of respondents and desirable by most others. It may come as something of a surprise to find ethnicity so far down the list of priorities (just 56% of respondents considered this essential). However, this might reflect reality in practice: often a child's ethnic heritage is so complex that an exact match cannot be

*Figure 8.1*
**Respondents' views on the relative importance of specific matching factors**

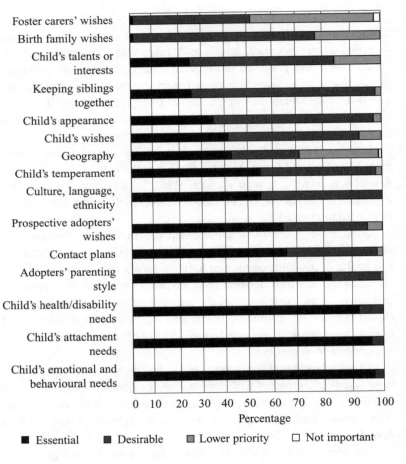

found and agencies will seek a match that is as close as possible, while ensuring that other needs are met and that placement is not delayed. Moreover, when a black or minority ethnic child has other special needs, it may be very difficult to find an ethnically matched family which can cope with these additional needs. The variation in approach is illustrated by the quotations below:

> We base matching on ethnic background and operate a "same-race" policy for adoption. Voluntary agency

> Difficult decisions sometimes have to be made. For example, if one cannot find an ideal match in relation to ethnicity, we might look at expanding boundaries so that a child is not kept waiting indefinitely for an ideal family that may never become available. Shire county

The issue of sibling group placement reveals that, while most respondents thought that placing siblings together was desirable for the majority of cases, only a quarter of respondents considered it essential.

There were very few areas of difference between the responses of local authority and voluntary agency representatives. Interestingly, more voluntary agencies than local authorities saw matching on the child's talents and interests as essential, but this difference was not statistically significant. In relation to geography (the distance between the placing agency and the adoptive home), 81 per cent of local authorities viewed this as an essential or desirable element in matching, while 65 per cent of voluntary agencies thought this factor less, or not at all, important (Fisher's Exact Test $p = .001$). This issue is perhaps of less importance to voluntary agencies, since families approved and supported by their staff will always live within their catchment area. Overall, this chart suggests that professionals bring to the linking and matching task a pragmatic approach, probably informed by research and practice wisdom, as well as by personal conviction.

## Responses to statements about linking and matching

Our final method of exploring professionals' views on matching was to offer a series of statements about practice. These statements were designed to tap into respondents' experience, attitudes and beliefs in relation to areas of adoption practice that continue to pose dilemmas for practitioners. In some cases, these statements were specifically aimed at testing opinion on particularly contentious issues.

The 28 statements were presented in random order in the question-naire, but to ease presentation, we have divided them into four broad groupings:

- matching considerations where children have behavioural and/or attachment problems;
- adopters' expectations;
- practice questions; and
- other issues, including contact, placement of sibling groups, disability and finance.

The exact wording of the questions in each area is reproduced in four charts (Figures 8.2 to 8.5), along with the frequency of responses for each. Throughout, the charts have been drawn to show agreement with the statement in white or light bars and disagreement in grey or black bars.

## Views on placing children with behavioural or attachment problems

None of the statements produced unanimity of response, although some commanded larger majorities than others. Thus, working from the top of Figure 8.2, it is clear that the majority of respondents agreed that children who have behavioural or attachment difficulties may fare better when adopters require less of them in the way of emotional commitment. Importantly, however, there were a few respondents who strongly disagreed with this view.

All respondents agreed that, in order to successfully parent children with attachment problems, adopters required specific training and support. This view is reinforced by the responses to the next statement asserting that 'most adopters are able to manage most children once they have been through the assessment and preparation process'. This statement drew quite a mixed response, which suggests that, for many adopters, the general preparation for adoption should only be a beginning and that further specific training, advice and support will often be necessary. Whether it is always on offer is another question, but at least one agency in our survey did mention that such further input was a part of their routine practice. The need for further assistance certainly ought to

*Figure 8.2*

**Respondents' views on statements about behaviour and attachment issues**

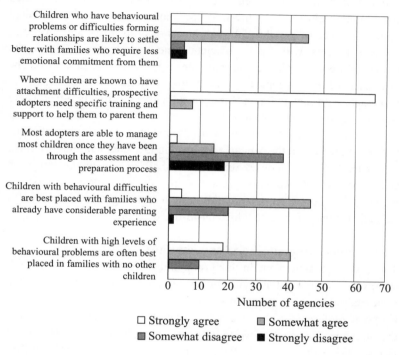

☐ Strongly agree     ▨ Somewhat agree
■ Somewhat disagree     ■ Strongly disagree

be considered, both as part of the preparation of the Adoption Placement Report and at the matching panel.

The two statements towards the bottom of Figure 8.2 cover the question of whether children with behavioural or attachment problems should be placed with child-free families or experienced parents. Some families, which are child-free at the time of applying to adopt, will have had previous parenting experience, but many will not. Overall, one can see advantages and disadvantages to each option, with child-free families having more time to commit to a child but often being untested in terms of their parenting skills. Families with parenting experience may have more confidence and resources to draw on but may feel de-skilled if strategies used previously do not seem to work with a placed child, or if they feel themselves to be failing if relationships do not develop as anticipated. If adoptive parents have other children in the home, then consideration must also be given to how those children may be affected by the presence of a child with high levels of problems – and indeed to whether parents will have sufficient time and energy to meet the individual needs of all the children (see, e.g. Quinton *et al*, 1998). The responses of professionals to these two comments were largely in agreement with such children being placed with child-free families. There was a slightly more mixed response to the statement about placing behaviourally difficult children with experienced parents, but still the majority agreed with the principle outlined in the statement. Interestingly, nearly half of the responses were "somewhat" in agreement with both statements, which would suggest that people who have successfully parented but no longer have children at home might be considered a valuable resource for some "difficult-to-place" children.

## Views concerning adopters' expectations

There were six statements in this group and, as is clear from Figure 8.3, there was a significant amount of consensus among professionals on the issues raised in these statements. The first concerns the "stretching" of adopters' preferences. This is a practice that has long been recognised in the literature and practice world as being unhelpful (see, e.g. Barth and Berry, 1988; Valentine *et al*, 1988; Valdez and McNamara, 1994; McRoy, 1999) and has often been included in discussions of disrupted adoptive placements. Almost all respondents to the survey agreed with the statement that "stretching" is associated with a higher risk of disruption. Almost all agreed too with the premise that it was very difficult to know how a child will respond to a new family. The majority agreed that adopters can be over-confident about the sorts of difficulties they will be able to manage. The responses to the two questions relating to adopters' reservations, taken together, clearly suggest that most professionals feel that reservations are to be taken seriously and would usually be an indicator that the link or match should not proceed. That said, many respondents agreed that adoptive parents can often manage children with disabilities, despite initial uncertainties on their part. The whole area of

*Figure 8.3*

**Respondents' views on statements about adopters' expectations**

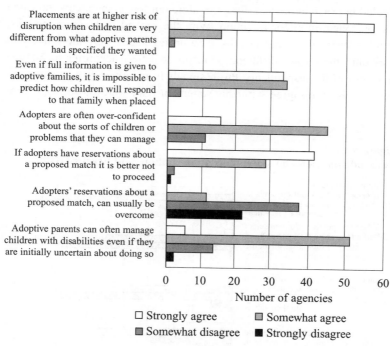

☐ Strongly agree     ☐ Somewhat agree

☐ Somewhat disagree     ■ Strongly disagree

reservation, hesitation and uncertainty on the part of adopters is one of degree. How these are responded to by professionals will be determined by their subjective interpretation of what adopters are saying – or not saying. The simple tick-box format used here cannot elicit the quality of detail required to take this further.

## Views concerning linking and practice issues

There was perhaps slightly more variation in the responses to some of the statements in this section, although there was a very strong tendency for people to agree with the first of these statements – namely, that children's social workers can be over-optimistic about the way in which children will settle in placement. The second and third statements from the top in

Figure 8.4 were designed to explore views about professional versus adopter-led methods of finding families. Here we found responses divided between agree and disagree, although few respondents indicated a strong view in either direction. With the second of these statements, which asserted that "matches made by professionals were more likely to work out", there was a difference in response pattern according to the type of agency of the respondents. Professionals from voluntary agencies were more likely to disagree with this statement than were those from local

*Figure 8.4*
**Respondents' views on statements about linking and practice issues**

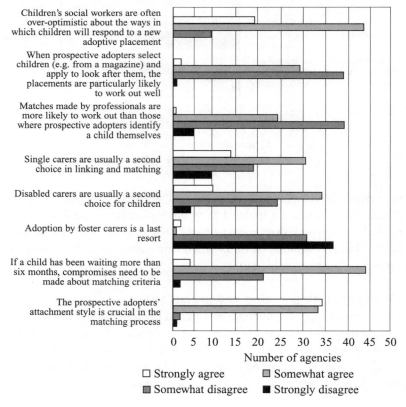

0    5    10    15    20    25    30    35    40    45    50
Number of agencies
☐ Strongly agree          ▨ Somewhat agree
▦ Somewhat disagree       ■ Strongly disagree

authorities. (Six per cent of voluntary adoption agency responses were in agreement, compared with 45 per cent of local authorities.)

The following two statements explored whether adoption professionals felt that single or disabled carers were viewed as a "second choice" for children. Here again, we found significant variation in response. For both of these statements, there was a difference between local authority and voluntary adoption agencies, with voluntary agencies far less likely to disagree with either statement. However, the number of voluntary agencies was small and calculating statistical probabilities would not be appropriate. As is clear from Figure 8.4, respondents were almost unanimous in disagreeing with the statement that "adoption by foster carers is a last resort".

A further practice issue in this section of the questionnaire was about whether or not the criteria used for family finding ought to be reconsidered if a child has been waiting more than six months for a family. Interestingly, while the majority thought that compromises should be made, a substantial minority did not. The final statement included here is about adopters' attachment styles and their importance in the matching process, and again we found almost universal agreement with the statement, which suggested that this is seen as a crucial part of the process.

### Views concerning other issues in adoption

In the final section of this part of the questionnaire, we explored a series of long-standing dilemmas facing those working in family placement. The responses of professionals to these statements are shown in Figure 8.5. Again, we note considerable variation in views on both of the questions relating to matching on ethnic or cultural needs, although once again relatively few respondents indicated strong views in either direction. There is a definite leaning towards the view that delays that may arise in the course of seeking an ethnically matched placement are unacceptable: 44 respondents strongly or somewhat agreed with the statement but a substantial minority (26) somewhat or strongly disagreed. Unfortunately, it is not possible to be absolutely certain whether these respondents were disagreeing with the premise that delay was unacceptable or the suggestion that prioritising ethnic needs can lead to delay.

Responses to the following statement, however, which suggested that 'making similar race placements is more important than maintaining existing attachments to current carers who wish to adopt the child' assist in our interpretation. Here, we found 30 respondents strongly or somewhat agreed and 42 somewhat or strongly disagreed with the statement. This, together with other discussion of this issue in this report, suggests that matching children's ethnic and cultural characteristics in an adoptive placement continues to be a primary concern for *some* professionals, even if this means a delay in securing a placement and/or disrupting existing attachments.

The next two statements address contact, once again, a highly contentious area. When we wrote the statements, we wanted to achieve wording that was quite provocative, which would provide responses that would give us a feel for how professionals in the adoption world viewed contact at the current time. From the chart, it is clear that the majority of respondents feel that high levels of birth parent contact can jeopardise placements, and also that there was a good deal of sympathy with the view that contact plans should be determined by adopters' views. We noted that voluntary agencies were particularly likely to agree with this statement, but so did nearly 40 per cent of local authorities.

We included four statements that touched on either the placement of sibling groups or interactions between children. Thinking first about maintaining or separating siblings for placement, the great majority agreed, and most of these strongly agreed, that siblings ought to be kept together unless there were contraindications to such a plan. Interestingly, this appears to contradict the findings outlined earlier when we asked respondents to prioritise matching factors (Figure 8.1). Equally, the majority disagreed that placing large groups of siblings together was unlikely to meet the needs of all the individual children – although the response here was somewhat less definitive. Respondents were divided over whether it is better to seek to place a disabled child separately, rather than to keep an able-bodied child waiting for placement. The next question was about the interaction between a placed child and other children in an adoptive family. Here there was almost universal, and strong, agreement that the quality of the interaction between children is often critical in determining the success of placements.

*Figure 8.5*

**Respondents' views on statements about other issues**

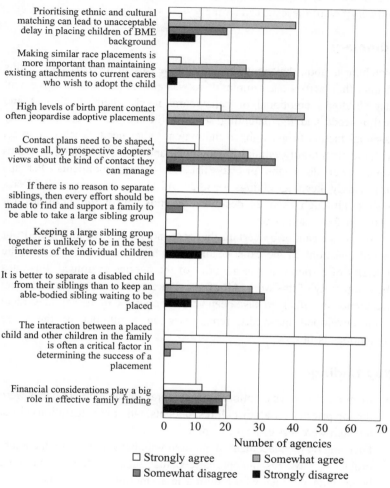

□ Strongly agree      ▤ Somewhat agree
▨ Somewhat disagree      ■ Strongly disagree

Our final statement in this "other issues" section was about money. Interestingly, this statement elicited the greatest diversity in response of all the statements. Perhaps not surprisingly, almost all the voluntary adoption agencies agreed with the statement that 'financial considerations play a big role in effective family finding', with half of them strongly agreeing. In contrast, only 36 per cent of local authorities agreed with this statement and very few of these agreed strongly.

## Summary

Matching is about balancing needs, and we saw in the first part of this chapter that, across our sample, there was almost unanimous agreement that children's emotional or behavioural needs, their attachment and health needs and the parenting style of the adopters were absolutely essential factors to get right in the match. Other needs, such as contact with the birth family, ethnicity, geography and even the children's wishes came lower down the priority list for some respondents. Perhaps surprisingly, keeping siblings together and taking account of children's wishes, although seen as desirable by most, were top priorities for relatively few respondents.

While we cannot be certain that respondents always interpreted our closed questions in the exact manner in which they were intended, the diversity of response to the majority of the queries examined illustrates the complexity of this work. All of our respondents were senior managers in adoption and likely to have been very experienced in their field, yet had often developed quite different views on a number of the more contentious issues.

## Key findings

- Meeting children's emotional, behavioural and attachment needs were the top priority for almost all respondents. Other considerations about a match were less critical for some.
- Focusing on the placement of children with behavioural or attachment problems, most respondents agreed that such children might settle better with families who required less emotional commitment from them and that the families would need specific training and support post-match and post-placement.
- Respondents tended to agree that children with behavioural or attachment problems are best placed in child-free families *and* with

adopters who already have parenting experience. The implication may be that slightly older adopters, whose own children had grown up, might be a valuable resource. Such families may also need less from the children in terms of attachment or emotional commitment.

- Exploring views about adopters' expectations produced a mixed picture. There was universal agreement that "stretching" of adopters' preferences puts placements at higher risk of difficulties. There was general agreement that adopters are often over-confident about the sorts of children they can manage, but if they do have reservations about a proposed match, it is probably better not to proceed.

- However, most respondents thought that adopters can often manage to parent children with disabilities, even if they are uncertain about this to start with.

- Looking at practice issues, the great majority of respondents agreed that children's workers are over-optimistic about the way in which children will settle in placement and that adopters' attachment style is important to the matching process. Most, but not all, agreed that the matching criteria need to be reviewed if no match is available after six months. Opinion was divided on whether adopter-led or professional-led matches were associated with better outcomes, and on whether disabled or single carers were a "second choice". Respondents were almost unanimous in disagreeing with the statement that 'adoption by foster carers is a last resort'.

- Responses to questions that focused on matching children's ethnic and cultural needs suggested that the principle of "same-race" placements was a priority for a substantial minority of professionals (about one-third), even if this was at the expense of existing attachments or involved a delay in identifying a suitable family.

# 9  The matching process in practice

About four in five of the agencies that responded to this section of our questionnaire (58 of 74) reported that their agency held the responsibility for making decisions about which families children should be placed with.

The preceding chapters have discussed the multitude of factors that professionals involved in adoption consider important in matching children and families. How then does matching operate in practice? A respondent wrote that one of the barriers to matching was 'juggling too many needs'. There are also uncertainties that make prediction difficult:

> *To be truthful, it is very difficult to be certain until the child is in placement. There are pleasant and unpleasant surprises. So many factors we can't prejudge.* Unitary authority

Similarly, Quinton (forthcoming) comments that some aspects of the fit between adoptive parents and children cannot be assessed before the new parents and children come together.

So how do agencies manage the task of selecting a family which might best meet the needs of a specific child? The answer is that there are a number of variations on a theme. One agency described the process thus:

> *A family finder is linked to a case as early as possible – sometimes at the parallel planning stage – so gains good overall picture of the child and needs in relation to adoption. She or he reads the case file and the CPR* [Child's Permanence Report], *meets the foster carer and child and draws up a matching needs profile.* [The family finder] *has access to information about families available within the county and regionally through consortium. The family finder would look at potential "in-house" families first and then the consortium. This is all done quite speedily because information is shared monthly between consortium agencies. Permission for expenditure to advertise is routinely given if there is a need to look further afield – no delays or*

*barriers preventing this. Matching is generally achieved within six months of the child's case having gone to panel. Once suitable families are identified, shortlisting down to two takes place. Both are visited, and if neither is suitable then social workers work down their list of families and shortlist the next most suitable and visit. A matching meeting, chaired by a senior manager, takes place to ensure the process has been properly followed and that the adopters meet the matching criteria. The adopters' social worker is invited to attend this meeting with the child's social worker and family finder.* Shire county

As in this example, in most agencies (76%), decisions about which families to proceed with were taken in a formal matching meeting.

*Figure 9.1*

**Frequency of attendance of different professionals and others at formal matching meetings**

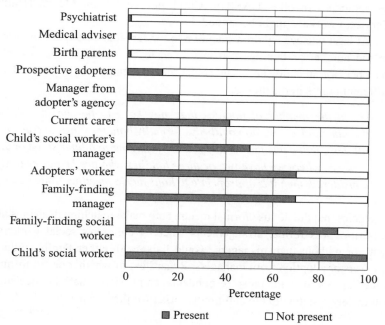

In the majority of agencies (60%), these meetings would generally include four to five of the individuals listed in Figure 9.1. Eight agencies reported that only two or three people would be present at these meetings; ten reported that meetings frequently involved six or more people. Several respondents pointed out that their procedures tended to be adaptable and responsive to circumstances, rather than having fixed routines.

> *A number of the above ticked as "no" MAY attend. It depends on how many families are being considered and specific issues relating to them or the child.* Unitary authority

> *Rather than routinely inviting people, we look to have those present who can offer appropriate information.*
> Unitary authority

Other respondents also stressed that there might be other people in those meetings if their presence was relevant to the child, for example, child psychologists or other CAMHS (Child and Adolescent Mental Health Services) workers might be invited.

At least one agency drew attention to the fact that cases vary in terms of the number of families that may need to be considered as possible matches for a child, and that sometimes meetings might be held at different points in the process:

> *Given the number of families that may have to be considered for certain children, we do not always formally hold meetings to consider all those that come through. If you are referring to a later stage in the process, where we have two or three families who are being seriously considered, then it is appropriate to hold such a meeting.* Shire county

Agencies that did not use formal meetings to make matching decisions all described less formal arrangements whereby children's social workers, with or without their managers, would liaise with either family-finding workers or adoption team managers. Regardless of whether or not formal meetings were held, most respondents emphasised that the decision ultimately rested with the children's worker (or their team).

*Discussion between family-finding worker and field social worker about prospective families and preferred family is then taken to a permanence planning meeting and an agreement to proceed is made.* Unitary authority

*Child's social worker is provided with brief profiles of all possible matches and can request full Form F for those they are interested in. Adopters' social workers will have profiles of children needing a match and will suggest families they consider suitable.* Shire county

In relation to the decision-making process, the proportion of people involved is very much the same as for formal meetings. The child's social worker is always involved (100%) in deciding which family to proceed with, as is their manager (91%), the family-finding worker (95%) and their manager (87%), plus the family's own support worker[14] in 75 per cent of the agencies. The potential adopters, who are not usually present at meetings, will, in 53 per cent of the agencies, be very much involved in the decision. However, 20 per cent of agencies said that prospective adopters would not be involved at all in the decision whether or not to match their family with a particular child. This may indicate different interpretations of the question, in that some respondents may be reflecting on earlier parts of the process. It seems somewhat surprising that adopters would not be at all involved in the matching, but quite likely that linking activities would proceed without their knowledge, and of course, the final decision as to which families to proceed with and whether a proposed match will be presented to the adoption panel will ultimately rest with professionals.

It was said that the child is almost always (98%) asked what the important priorities would be for them in matching. Indeed, a few agencies reported that children of an appropriate age and ability will attend their approval panel to talk about the sort of family they would like. However, most agencies (76%) would generally not encourage a child's involvement in deciding which family to proceed with.

---

[14] Prospective adoptive families will always have a named worker, allocated by the agency responsible for their assessment and approval. The family's agency may, or may not, also be responsible for the child.

Of course, knowing that agencies have formal meetings and knowing the usual composition of those meetings does not really allow us to understand what happens in those gatherings: what is being considered or discussed and in what depth by those present. It is not realistic to try to gather this sort of information from a self-completion questionnaire. However, it is an area that the second stage of this research will focus on in some detail.

## Sharing information about a child with prospective adopters

Adopters need to know a good deal about a child in order to be able to make an informed decision about whether they feel they will be able to parent him or her. In the past, substantial criticism has been aimed at social workers and agencies for not providing adequate information to adoptive families (Quinton *et al*, 1998). There has also been debate about how much adopters are really able to take in at the point at which a potential placement is being discussed, and the extent to which they may focus on "what they want to hear" rather than the full array of inform-ation presented. Inadequate information has been implicated in the disruption of adoptive placements (Evan B Donaldson Adoption Institute, 2004; Selwyn *et al*, 2006), and at least one council has been prosecuted for not supplying key information (Dyer, 2002). This emphasises the import-ance of not only providing full information but also trying to deliver it in a way that will engage adopters and encourage them to see the whole child.

The timing of information giving may also be important. Facts that might cause alarm bells to ring for adopters in the early stages may be accommodated by them if they come to light some way down the line, when they have already made an emotional commitment or investment in a particular child.

We were interested, therefore, in finding out not only in what format information was provided to prospective adopters, but also at what stages of the process. We offered a list of possible means of offering adopters information about children and asked respondents to indicate whether, in their agency, this source of information was shared with adopters "in the linking process", "after linking but before a match was approved", "after a match was approved" or "both before and after a match was approved" (see Tables 9.1 and 9.2).

For the purposes of the report, we divide the possible sources of information into written reports or other recorded material and meetings with people. To begin with written reports, we found that all agencies used the Child's Permanence Report (CPR) as a mechanism for presenting information to prospective families (see Table 9.1). This, in its full form at least, should provide the fullest, digestible description of the child and his or her experiences to date. About half of the agencies reported using this with adoptive families, principally during the linking process, but all ensured that it was seen prior to the matching decision. About 85 per cent of agencies indicated that they shared video images of children, and again this format was frequently used during linking as well as later in the process. Children's medical and other assessment reports were also made available to adopters by all the agencies, and once again were used by about a third of agencies during linking as well as later on.

Children's life story books were widely used as means of sharing information with adopters, but many agencies (56%) reserved these documents for use after a match had been approved. Sight of the child's case file was available to families in 56 per cent of agencies and, again, was usually reserved until after the matching panel – although almost half

*Table 9.1*
**Frequency and point of use of written material to inform adopters**

| | Linking stage (%) | Before match) (%) | After match (%) | Both before and after (%) | Not used (%) |
|---|---|---|---|---|---|
| View CPR | 53 | 9 | – | 38 | 0 |
| Video/DVD | 34 | 22 | 4 | 25 | 15 |
| Medical/other assessment reports | 33 | 30 | 6 | 31 | 0 |
| Life story book | – | 13 | 60 | 21 | 6 |
| Case file | 5 | 5 | 28 | 18 | 44 |

of the agencies did not share case files with prospective adopters. The holding back of these more personal and identifying documents until after the match is approved is understandable from the point of view of privacy and confidentiality, should things not proceed as planned.

The other main means of imparting information to adopters was by offering the opportunity to speak to others who knew the child. Table 9.2 illustrates the options that were presented in the questionnaire, along with the responses.

*Table 9.2*
**Frequency and point of use of meetings with people to inform adopters**

|  | Linking stage (%) | Before match (%) | After match (%) | Both before and after (%) | Not used % |
|---|---|---|---|---|---|
| Talk to specialists involved with the child (paediatrician or psychiatrist) | 23 | 33 | 1 | 43 | 0 |
| Talk to teachers or educational psychologist about learning needs | 21 | 20 | 17 | 41 | 1 |
| Meet with foster carers | 37 | 25 | 1 | 37 | 0 |
| Meet with birth family | – | 4 | 91 | 4 | 1 |
| Life Appreciation Day or equivalent | 6 | 12 | 34 | 5 | 43 |
| Unseen viewing | 2 | 10 |  | 2 | 86 |

As is clear from Table 9.2 (and Table 9.1), the majority of authorities responding to this section of the questionnaire exploited as many means as possible to ensure that prospective adopters have opportunities to speak to people who know the child from different perspectives – although there was some variation in terms of when these opportunities were made available. Meetings with birth family members almost invariably took place after the match was approved. Opportunities were made available for prospective adopters to meet the children's foster carers, paediatrician or child psychiatrist and teachers at the linking stage in between 21 and 37 per cent of cases.

Life Appreciation Days, also known as Child Appreciation Days and by a variety of other terms, entail inviting adopters to a gathering of individuals who know the child in a variety of different settings and from different perspectives. The organisation and implementation of these meetings has been described previously in the practice literature (see e.g. Cousins, 2003) and proponents of this practice believe that this approach helps to provide a fuller and richer picture of the child and his or her experiences to date. Briefly, an extended meeting will focus on exploring the child, his or her behaviour, interaction patterns and needs in different contexts. This very direct method of sharing knowledge and information was less frequently used than one-to-one contacts, but was used, at least on occasion, by 57 per cent of the agencies, and several other respondents mentioned that they were interested in (or were in the process of trying to organise) such events. Their use was seen as particularly important for older children or those with more complex histories. For the most part, these events occurred after a match had been approved.

*Child Appreciation Meetings give an opportunity to focus on the child in detail and give the adopters as much information as possible.* Shire county

*Life Appreciation Days help form a view about the child's past and the implications for the future.* Shire county

Last on this list is "unseen viewings". This is where prospective adopters have sight of a child in an environment that is comfortable for the child but without him or her knowing who the adopters are or why they are there. This practice was rarely used by the agencies responding to the questionnaire. However, one agency that did use this method wrote:

*We are one of the few agencies who still do "blind" or "unseen" viewings of children prior to linking. In inter-agency placements we*

*are often criticised for this practice. Our adopter feedback tells us that
without this practice it becomes a "paper exercise" and there is no
consideration of emotional chemistry. Our placements seldom disrupt,
potential disruptions happen pre-panel when the child is unaware.
The CSCI* [Commission for Social Care Inspection] *has criticised this
practice and needs to be made aware of user feedback and how this
practice is child-led.* Shire county

We asked whether agencies had developed any other methods for ensuring
information reached adopters: very few said they had done so. One or two
reported liaison with a child psychologist or the release of specialist court
reports.

## Specific ways of working in linking and matching

Disappointingly, in view of the interest in this area, only ten agencies said
they had developed specific approaches or tools in relation to linking
and matching, and the descriptive information provided in response to
this specific question was often scant. An additional two agencies had
provided relevant information in response to an earlier question.

Essentially, agencies that did respond discussed formalised meetings
for making decisions about which family to proceed with and/or how a
particular family might meet the needs of a specific child.

*The permanency core group will identify families that may be able
to meet children's needs using matching criteria tool. Shortlist of
families will be visited and formal matching meeting later held if they
are considered to be a good match for the child.* Shire county

One agency wrote about a development specific to that agency:

*Prior to any approach being made to adopters, we always hold a
referral meeting involving the child's social worker, child's family
finder, foster carer (if possible)* [and] *two workers from our agency
who represent the prospective adopters. Adopters are given minutes
from that meeting in addition to the CPR and child's medical record.*
Voluntary agency

The use of grids or matrices that compare children's needs with adopters' skills or qualities, or a similar technique to explore risks and vulnerabilities, was also specifically mentioned by four or five agencies.

*We have a list of all the children in the permanency planning process and* [another list] *of all of our adopters and assessments underway. When we identify potential matches, we use a matching matrix to look at the child's needs and the family's ability to meet them. We use this if there is a choice too. We do have a database that includes a matching tool, but this is not really used.* Metropolitan area

With the specific permission of the local authorities involved, we have reproduced two examples of these instruments in Appendix C. Each takes a slightly different approach but both provide a structured method for considering an array of information in an objective manner. However, it is worth noting that in discussion with other adoption managers, one told us that workers had stopped using the matrix in her authority as it added to the amount of paperwork and they reached the same conclusion whether or not they used it. Another commented that the tick-box format of the matrix could lead to two families having the same number of points, so that workers still had to use their judgement to make a final decision.

The final approach mentioned in this section was the use of structured instruments to itemise children's behavioural and emotional difficulties, for example the Strengths and Difficulties Questionnaire (Goodman, 1997).

Of course, while relatively few agencies provided information in this section, a good deal of information about relevant practice development was evident in other sections of this report. Nonetheless, it appears that matching as a task is relatively unexplored and conceptually under-developed. As Quinton (forthcoming) comments, this may be partly because matching tries to put together parents and children, each of whom have unique characteristics and capacities, whereas research tells us about averages and probabilities across groups of parents and children. In the words of one of our respondents:

*I think that we are lacking a research base on linking – it is usually done through staff feeling that a couple will provide a suitable family.*

*General linking features fit but "guts" often play a large part!* Unitary authority

## Summary

Overall, it can be seen that there are a variety of approaches to the actual matching task. From the closed questions in this section of the survey, we established that the great majority of agencies used some form of formalised meeting to make decisions about a match, but the accompanying narrative clarified that the timing and the format of these meetings was not uniform. A substantial minority do not use such matching meetings.

Not only is there variation across agencies in terms of their procedures, there is frequently variation within agencies depending on the case. Much will depend on the complexity of a child's needs as to how much detailed discussion is required. Equally, it is clear that the task will be very different if there are 20 or so families who may be able to parent a healthy baby in comparison with a child who is older or has a disability, where it may be a struggle to locate one suitable family.

## Key findings

- Seventy per cent of agencies used a formalised meeting to discuss matches, although there was some variation in the point at which these were used in the linking and matching process, and they were not used in all cases.
- In many agencies, the professionals represented at these meetings varied according to the characteristics of the case. Other agencies relied on less formal arrangements to discuss matches.
- The decision about which family to proceed with ultimately rested with the child's allocated social worker.
- Children were almost always asked what sort of family they would like, but they were not usually involved in decisions about which family was chosen.
- Agencies used a range of methods to provide information about children to prospective adopters, including sight of the child's CPR, a

video or DVD of the child, and medical and other reports. In many agencies, these materials were available to families before the matching panel meeting.

- The child's life story book was a further source of information in almost all agencies, although this was usually held back until after the match had been considered at panel.
- Around half of respondents reported that adopters would also have sight of the case file – again, after the matching panel.
- Almost all agencies offered the opportunity for families to meet with other professionals involved with the child and with foster carers prior to the matching panel.
- Meetings of adopters with birth family members occurred in all agencies (although it is not clear that this would be in all cases) but usually happened after a match had been approved. Child Appreciation Days were *sometimes* arranged in around 57 per cent of agencies and, again, tended to occur after a match had been approved.
- "Unseen viewings" of the child were used by only 13 per cent of agencies, but one proponent of the practice felt strongly that this was helpful to prospective adopters.
- In comparison with other stages of the adoption process, practice in matching seemed relatively undeveloped. Apart from the use of Child Appreciation Days (or the equivalent), the only significant development identified by the survey was the use of grids or matrices to provide a systematic and unbiased means of checking children's needs against the strengths and characteristics of potential families.

# 10 The adoption panel

A critical part of the adoption process is the operation of adoption panels. According to the Adoption Agencies Regulations (2005), each adoption agency must have a panel, although there is provision for some agencies to share panel responsibilities between themselves. With the implementation of these regulations, the membership of adoption panels is quite prescribed, as is the way they operate. Essentially, adoption panels are able to consider the evidence submitted to them in order to make recommendations about:

- whether a child should be placed for adoption;
- whether a family should be approved to become adopters;
- whether a particular child should be matched and placed with a particular family.

In some agencies, panels have an expanded role and will also consider a variety of other permanent placement options for looked after children, and some will consider approval of foster carers alongside adopters. In other authorities, these latter responsibilities will be considered by separate panels.

Because the role of adoption panels is so pivotal in the adoption process, we were keen to include some questions about the ways in which they operate. We also wished to explore respondents' views on any changes that had occurred since the implementation of the new regulations. Seventy-three respondents contributed to this section of the survey (56 local authorities and 17 voluntary adoption agencies).

We began by exploring the types of cases that were considered by adoption panels. All but one of the agencies operated their own adoption panel. As illustrated in Table 10.1, panels varied, as outlined above, in terms of the sorts of applications that they would consider. The largest group of agencies, accounting for over half of those responding, might be thought of as having traditional adoption panels, dealing with adoption of children and the matching and approval of prospective adopters. However,

*Table 10.1*

**Types of cases considered by the panel that considers adoption for looked after children**

|  | *No.* | *%* |
|---|---|---|
| Adoption of looked after children and approval of adopters | 37 | 51 |
| Adoption of looked after children and approval of adopters and foster carers | 6 | 8 |
| All permanence decisions for looked after children | 4 | 5 |
| All permanence decisions for looked after children and approval of adopters | 8 | 11 |
| All permanence decisions and approval of both adopters and foster carers | 1 | 1 |
| Approval of adopters only (voluntary adoption agencies) | 15 | 21 |
| Approval of adopters and foster carers only (voluntary adoption agencies) | 2 | 3 |
| **Total** | **73** | **100** |

there was considerable variation in responsibilities amongst the remaining agencies.

## The independent Chair

Under the Adoption Agencies Regulations 2005, it became mandatory for panels to have an independent Chair. We wanted to know whether respondents had detected any differences in the way their panels operated as a result of this change.

About two-thirds of the respondents (65%) indicated that the change had been positive, a small minority (8%) had rather mixed views and 21 per cent felt that this had made little difference in practice. A number of agencies commented that they had long worked with an independent Chair, so this may account for many of those who noted little change. Although there was an opportunity for respondents to elaborate on their answers, very few did so. We have reproduced a few of the comments that illustrate the mainstream of opinion but also, in some cases, highlight other issues.

*Figure 10.1*
**Views on the independent Chair**

> *We have two adoption panels and one has always had an independent Chair. We have had some excellent chairing by leading elected members prior to the requirement for independence – also some far less good experiences in the more distant past. I do not feel independence is the key feature linked to quality – but it does help to reinforce the separation of panel and agency in a healthy way.*
>
> Shire county

> *We have always had independent Chairs and it is very much dependent on personality how panel is conducted.*
>
> Voluntary agency

> *There has always been an independent Chair since I have been in post so it is hard to give a clear response. My overall impression is that it has raised the standard of panel discussion and hence recommendations.*
>
> Metropolitan area,
> NW England

## Panel activity and depth of scrutiny

The frequency with which panels met to consider either the adoption of children or the approval of adoptive families varied between four and 88 times a year. As expected, there was a strong positive correlation ($r = 0.832$) between the number of children placed and the frequency with which panels sat.

There has been some debate in the practice press about the role of adoption panels and the extent to which members scrutinise the materials submitted to them. We asked agencies first to indicate the length of time that would be spent, on average, reviewing each type of case in which we were interested.

*Figure 10.2*

**Average time taken to consider three types of adoption panel recommendation**

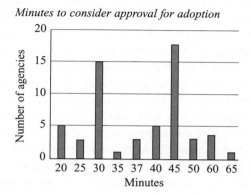

*Minutes to consider approval for adoption*

*Minutes to consider a matching recommendation*

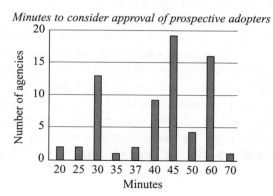

*Minutes to consider approval of prospective adopters*

As is clear from the charts in Figure 10.2, there was considerable variation across agencies, with the maximum times recorded (60–70 minutes) being at least three times longer than the minimum (20 minutes) in each case. While there were moderate correlations within agencies between the times taken over various types of case (r = 0.5 to 0.7), there was no association with the type of agency, the number of cases considered or the frequency of panel meetings. Of course, allocating only 20 minutes does not necessarily mean that the scrutiny is any less. Panel operation may be such that members do most of their considering prior to a panel meeting and thus the time spent in discussion may be more focused and concise (see *Ways of working with the adoption panel* below). However, it seems unlikely that panels that operate so swiftly would be able to accommodate some of the more recent developments that were reported, such as inviting those whose cases were being considered to attend in person. This approach was seen as a very positive move by those using it (again, see *Ways of working with the adoption panel* below).

A second potential indicator of depth of scrutiny might be the extent to which the panel referred cases back to the agency for further inform-ation or disagreed with the proposed plan. This again is not a clear-cut indication, as it might equally say a good deal about the quality of the information originally provided to the panel. (In this context, it is worth noting that Selwyn and her colleagues (2008) found that 17 per cent of the Child's Permanence Reports (CPRs) in their study were poorly written, with gaps in chronologies or sections incomplete.) Nevertheless, we asked respondents to estimate the proportion of cases that were either sent back for further information or not agreed at all by the panel. The responses to these questions are to be found in Table 10.2.

As can be seen, there was again a wide variation in these estimates, particularly so where the panel was considering whether or not a child should be placed for adoption (where from 0 to 30% of cases were sent back for further information and between 0 and 18% of cases were not agreed by panels). It is possible that these figures are inflated for some agencies because they are dealing with very small numbers of children being presented to panel. For example, if there were only ten such cases being considered in a year and three of these children comprised one

*Table 10.2*
**The proportion of cases sent back or not agreed by panel**

|  | Sent back for further information | Proportion not agreed by panel |
|---|---|---|
| Should be placed for adoption recommendations | 0 to 30% (Mean = 7.8 sd = 5.6) | 0 to 18% (Mean 4.05, sd = 4.9) |
| Matching recommendations | 0 to 10% (Mean 2.1, sd = 2.3) | 0 to 10% (Mean = 1.4, sd = 2.2) |
| Approval of prospective adopters | 0 to 10% (Mean 3.7, sd = 3.0) | 0 to 10% (Mean = 2.4 sd = 2.7) |

sibling group about whom the panel had further questions, this would produce a return rate of 30 per cent. That said, statistical tests did not support this hypothesis. The correlation between the proportion of adoption recommendations returned for further information was positively, rather than negatively, associated with the number of children placed each year, although only modestly so ($r = 0.52$, $p<0.05$). This suggests that the more cases considered by a panel, the greater the proportion likely to be sent back. Data were available for relatively few of the busier panels but there was a tendency for these agencies to report a higher proportion of papers being returned with requests for further information, particularly when the panel was considering whether a child should be placed for adoption. There was a similar, although less marked, pattern in relation to matching recommendations that were questioned by panel (but here the correlations were very small: $r = 0.3$). This might indicate that the more experienced panels had the confidence to insist on high-quality paperwork before recommendations were made.

The majority of respondents (84%) indicated that panel members were usually, although not always, in agreement with the recommendations made about matches, with just five per cent of panels always reaching unanimous decisions. (The remaining panels did not consider matches.)

Adoption panels make recommendations rather than decisions about matches between children and families: the final decision rests with the agency decision maker. We therefore wanted to know how often the recommendations made by panel were overturned when sent for ratification. Over half of the agencies responding to this section of the survey (51%) reported that no recommendations had been overturned in the last three years. In a third of the agencies this had occurred, but only very occasionally. The remaining agencies either did not know or their panels did not consider matching recommendations. We invited respondents to provide some detail on situations where decisions were not ratified and a few did so. The details of these cases suggested that this tended to happen more in relation to the approval of adopters, and one or two of the descriptions mentioned the involvement of the Independent Review Mechanism (IRM). The IRM is a review process, conducted by a panel, which prospective adopters can use when they have been told that their adoption agency does not propose to approve them as suitable to adopt a child (www.irm-adoption.org.uk). The IRM was launched by BAAF in 2004 on behalf of the Department for Education and Skills (now the Department for Children, Schools and Families) and has been extended to consider the cases of foster carers.

*When the IRM recommended approval, the agency decision maker accepted their recommendation, thus overturning the original panel's view. This concerned foster carers going on to adopt children already placed.* Metropolitan area

This second example illustrates how changes in circumstances can sometimes come into play.

*On one occasion the decision maker overturned the panel's recommendation not to place a third child in a family where they had taken an older sibling but at time of matching were pregnant with a birth child.* Metropolitan area

## Ways of working with the adoption panel

Finally, when asked whether agencies had developed particular ways of working with the adoption panel, nearly 60 per cent of agencies said they had done so. Not all agencies proceeded to give us details of these new methods, but many did. The majority of responses reflected the development of packs, checklists or practice guidance tools for use by panel members in making their decisions and several mentioned the development of training programmes, often run jointly with social work practitioners. One agency mentioned the establishment of a designated adviser role, which entailed no other distracting responsibilities. Another talked about the involvement of the panel Chair in quarterly business meetings and strategic planning for the adoption service.

Other responses included the preparation of information sheets for individuals attending panel and setting up feedback systems to seek views on the operation of the panel from social workers, prospective adopters and children, where appropriate.

Some agencies wrote about the attendance at panel of prospective adopters and one or two mentioned the attendance of birth parents or children if they were old enough.

*. . . Birth parents are invited to the adoption panel at the point that the plan for adoption is being considered and can give their views on the kind of family they would want for their child if adoption is the chosen plan.* Unitary authority

*Also children of an appropriate age are invited to attend the adoption panel at the point that the plan for adoption is being considered. This does not happen very often as most of the children we place are pre-school.* Unitary authority

*Prospective adopters attend panel for the entire discussion at approval and match and, where appropriate, young people.* Unitary authority

One voluntary agency emphasised that panel members were asked to come to the meeting having already prepared their comments on the papers.

*We ask panel members to think of strengths and areas for further work/concern in advance, and bring to the panel in writing.* Voluntary agency

One or two agencies described appraisals for panel members and, presumably recognising the potentially distressing nature of the material presented to panel members, one agency spoke of a system of "debriefing" that was offered at the end of each meeting and also a support network for panel members.

## Key findings

- Agencies varied in the way their adoption panels were organised and the types of recommendations that were considered; that is, some panels considered all types of permanence decisions while others focused on adoption only. Voluntary agencies, of course, considered only the approval of adopters.
- On the whole, respondents felt that the move to an independent Chair of the adoption panel had been positive, although several stressed that the quality of chairing depended on the individual Chair and his or her abilities rather than independence *per se*.
- There was substantial variation between agencies in the frequency with which panels might request further information or refuse to make a particular recommendation. The rate of requests for further information in relation to adoption recommendations was associated with the number of children placed for adoption, which might, in turn, relate to the panel's confidence in demanding high-quality paperwork before making a decision.
- It was relatively rare that panel recommendations were not agreed by the agency decision maker. Where this had happened, it appeared to reflect quite unusual circumstances. The number of cases in which a recommendation was not ratified was not associated with the number of children placed for adoption.
- Examples of practice development in terms of working with the panel included the use of checklists and guidance tools, as well as joint training for panel members. Respondents also mentioned the use of feedback systems for social workers, adopters and, sometimes, children. Some agencies spoke of compiling information packs for individuals attending panel, and one expected written comments to be prepared in advance of the meeting. One or two agencies mentioned

that children, when old enough, were encouraged to attend the panel when the plan for adoption was being considered.

# 11 Estimated costs of adoption activities

An important component of this national survey was to make broad estimates of the costs associated with adoption activities. Just one study has been completed recently that considers adoption costs (Selwyn *et al*, 2006) and there is one review that focuses on commissioning for adoption services (Deloitte, 2006). Therefore, improving the evidence base on costs for both providers and commissioners is an important goal for research.

We used data provided for this national survey to estimate the costs of teams involved in adoption and to calculate the costs of four main processes undertaken by these teams: assessing a child; assessing a prospective adoptive family; profiling a child for adoption; and talking to children and families as part of the linking process.

The first section of this chapter describes the methodology used and compares the agencies that provided sufficient cost-related data – that is, those agencies used in calculating costs – with those in the full sample of survey respondents for regional location, type of authority and time spent on various activities. It is important to remember that here we are dealing with only a sub-sample of the respondents, around 40 agencies, so while the "costs sample" is reasonably representative of the full sample, some of the ranges and means presented may differ slightly from those found in other parts of the report.

## Cost estimation methodology

The national survey allowed a broad-brush approach to estimating the costs of adoption activities, one in which we could ask agencies for some basic information about numbers of children and staff as well as expenditure and time use. This survey approach would provide data on the *service-level* costs of adoption. Previous experience with this type of data collection exercise suggested that about half of the respondents to the survey would be able to provide these data (Beecham *et al*, 2003, 2007).

These cross-sectional data will be complemented by the in-depth data collected in the second stage of this study, which takes a *child-level* approach focusing on the costs of all the supports particular children receive as they go through the adoption process.

Within the survey, we included questions about the staffing and expenditure for the team that undertook adoption activities, the amount of time spent on adoption activities in relation to other social work activities, and the number of children adopted or going through the various stages associated with adoption in the last year. We were also interested in the time committed to particular adoption activities: assessing a child, assessing an adoptive parent, profiling a child and talking to people as part of the linking process. Our approach here was to ask about *the last child/adoptive parent* considered. This would give us data from several agencies. We have no reason to assume that the resulting set of cases would not reflect the range of children being placed for adoption in all those agencies over the year. Linking our questions to the last event was a simpler approach than asking for "typical" or "on average" practice. As we saw in earlier chapters, social workers feel that the children they deal with are all so different and receive such different levels of support that identifying patterns across children is very difficult. Our data amply illustrate the tremendous variation in time spent undertaking ostensibly similar activities.

The costs presented in the following sections use the data that agencies reported in the survey. There were not sufficient research resources to undertake any follow-up calls to confirm or collect extra data. The findings reflect what the authorities told us about expenditure and budgets rather than the economic ideal of consistently estimated costs following the principles of long-run marginal opportunity costs.[15]

---

[15]  The marginal cost is the cost of supporting one extra child. Use of short-run marginal costs may give the impression that however many extra children need support, the current set of services has the capacity to support them. But as there is a limit to the number of children that can be "squeezed in", long-run marginal costs recognise the financial implications of the necessary expansion. For more information, see, for example, Beecham, 2000.

However, we have explored the data carefully to check that, broadly speaking, salary data are in line with expectations for that group of professionals and national data, and that the proportion of each team's expenditure absorbed by salaries is in line with our expectations. Thus, our checks have focused on internal consistency within each team or agency and within the dataset.

## Identifying the "costs sample"

Staff members are the core of any social work team. The mix and number of staff are also important in estimating and validating cost information because staff costs (salaries, on-costs and the like) generally comprise a high proportion of total costs. Often this can be in the range of 65–80 per cent (Curtis and Netten, 2006). Seventy agencies provided information on the number of full-time-equivalent staff in the various broad categories requested in the survey.

The mean total number of full-time-equivalent (fte) staff for these 70 adoption agencies was 14.0 (sd 10), with the smallest team having just 2.5 fte staff and the largest having 67 staff members. Table 11.1 also shows that the mean total number of fte staff per team was similar for local authorities and voluntary agencies, with both having an average of 14 staff members ($p = 0.871$). There was also little difference between the local authorities and voluntary agencies in terms of the balance of staff groups.

To estimate the costs of adoption teams, respondents to this national survey were asked two overarching questions about their finances:

- What is the total budget for your adoption service?
- What is the total expenditure on staff salaries?

Forty-one of the responding agencies provided sufficient costs information for our calculations: 30 local authorities and 11 voluntary agencies. Of this group, 39 agencies also provided information on their staffing profile. Table 11.2 shows that those agencies providing sufficient cost information appear to have slightly larger teams on average (15.8 vs 11.7 for the 29 teams with staffing data but which could provide no cost

*Table 11.1*
**Staffing profile for local authority (LA) and voluntary adoption agency (VAA) teams**

| Staff group | LA | | | VAA | | | All teams | | |
|---|---|---|---|---|---|---|---|---|---|
| | *Mean. no. fte* | *Range* | *No. teams* | *Mean no. fte* | *Range* | *No. teams* | *Mean no. fte* | *Range* | *No. teams* |
| Senior manager | 0.79 | 0–2 | 53 | 1.08 | 0–5 | 17 | 0.86 | 0–5 | 70 |
| Team leader | 1.48 | 0–6 | 54 | 1.37 | 0–5 | 17 | 1.45 | 0–6 | 71 |
| Panel adviser (if not otherwise included) | 0.39 | 0–4 | 52 | 0.1 | 0–1 | 17 | 0.32 | 0–4 | 69 |
| Qualified social worker | 7.38 | 0–33.5 | 53 | 6.49 | 0.5–20.5 | 17 | 7.16 | 0–33.5 | 70 |
| Unqualified social worker | 0.64 | 0–8 | 52 | 0.8 | 0–10 | 17 | 0.68 | 0–10 | 69 |
| Admin/clerical staff | 2.60 | 0–21 | 53 | 3.56 | 0–10 | 17 | 2.83 | 0–21 | 70 |
| Other posts | 0.45 | 0–4 | 53 | 1.01 | 0–10 | 17 | 0.59 | 0–10 | 70 |
| **Total** | **13.93** | **4.5–67** | **51[1]** | **14.43** | **2.5–43** | **17[1]** | **14.06** | **2.5–67** | **68[1]** |

*Notes:* [1]Number of teams for whom data were recorded for all categories of staff

information), particularly among qualified social workers. However, the difference in the total number of fte staff was not statistically significant between these two groups. This suggests that teams in our costs sample are similar in size to those for whom costs were not available. Within the costs sample, there was no statistically significant difference between local authorities and voluntary agencies in the number of fte staff.[16]

Table 11.2
**Comparison of the staff profile**

| Staff group | With costs data | | | Without costs data | | |
|---|---|---|---|---|---|---|
| | Average no. fte | Range | No. teams | Average no. fte | Range | No. teams |
| Senior manager | 0.91 | 0–5 | 41 | 0.78 | 0–2 | 29 |
| Team leader | 1.59 | 0–5 | 41 | 1.26 | 0–6 | 30 |
| Panel adviser (if not otherwise included) | 0.2 | 0–2 | 40 | 0.49 | 0–4 | 29 |
| Qualified social worker | 8.48 | 2–33.5 | 40 | 5.41 | 0–14 | 30 |
| Unqualified social worker | 0.65 | 0–10 | 40 | 0.72 | 0–8 | 29 |
| Admin/clerical staff | 3.32 | 0–21 | 40 | 2.18 | 0–7 | 30 |
| Other posts | 0.47 | 0–3 | 40 | 0.74 | 0–10 | 30 |
| **Total** | **15.79** | **5.35–67** | **39[1]** | **11.72[1]** | **2.5–25** | **29[1]** |

Notes: [1] Number of teams for whom data were recorded for all categories of staff

Table 11.3 shows the proportion of responding agencies in the costs sample from each region or by authority type, and similar data for the full sample. Looking at the regional data, for example, the costs sample has a smaller proportion of local authorities from NW England than the full sample (3% compared to 11%) but a higher proportion of the cost sample responses come from the West Midlands (17% compared to 10%). Looking at respondents by authority type, however, the picture for the cost sample and the full sample is very similar. Notably, voluntary agencies are

---

[16] Both parametric and non-parametric statistical tests have been used. Note that where sectoral comparisons are made within the costs sample, the sample sizes are small.

*Table 11.3*
**Comparing region and authority type**

| LA region | % (n) agencies | |
| --- | --- | --- |
| | *With costs* | *Full sample* |
| E Midlands / Eastern | 13% (4) | 10% (7) |
| London | 20% (6) | 18% (13) |
| NE England / Yorks & Humber | 13% (4) | 15% (11) |
| NW England | 3% (1) | 11% (8) |
| SE England | 13% (4) | 17% (12) |
| SW England | 10% (3) | 13% (9) |
| Wales | 10% (3) | 7% (5) |
| West Midlands | 17% (5) | 10% (7) |
| All LAs | 43% (30) | 100% (72) |
| *LA type* | % (n) agencies | |
| Shire county | 23% (7) | 26% (19) |
| Unitary authority | 30% (9) | 29% (21) |
| Metropolitan | 17% (5) | 19% (14) |
| Inner London | 10% (3) | 7% (5) |
| Outer London | 13% (4) | 11% (8) |
| Welsh agency | 7% (2) | 7% (5) |
| All VAAs | 65% (11) | 100% (17) |

over-represented in the costs sample which contains 11 of the 17 respondents in the full sample (65%); the proportion is lower for local authorities where just 30 of all 72 responding agencies were in the cost sample (42%).

## The costs of adoption teams

One further adjustment was made to the costs sample. This was to reflect the fact that in some agencies the teams undertook a wider range of activities, perhaps other family-finding work or other social work tasks with children and their families. We asked agencies to report the proportion of time the team spent on adoption activities.

Three local authorities included in the costs sample did not provide this information. Of the remaining 38 agencies, 31 spent all of their time on adoption activities, two each spent 95, 90 and 85 per cent of their time on adoption activities, with one team recording just 50 per cent. Table 11.4 compares these data with teams for whom cost data were not available and for all teams. Those providing cost data are more likely to have reported that their team spent 100 per cent of their time on adoption activities (82% vs 61%), although this may just reflect the relatively higher proportion of voluntary agencies that provided cost-related information. Sixty-nine per cent of local authorities answering this question reported that their team spent 100 per cent of their time on adoption activities compared to 82 per cent of voluntary agencies.

*Table 11.4*
**Proportion of time spent on adoption activities**

| *% time spent on adoption activities* | *No. adoption agencies' teams (%)* | | |
|---|---|---|---|
| | *With cost data* | *Without cost data* | *All teams* |
| 40%–50% | 1 | 2 | 3 |
| 75%–80% | 0 | 5 | 5 |
| 85%–90% | 4 | 0 | 4 |
| 95% | 2 | 4 | 6 |
| 100% | 31 (82%) | 17 (61%) | 48 (73%) |
| No. teams reporting % time | 38/41 | 28/48 | 66/89 |

These overarching data on the time spent on adoption activities are important for the cost estimation task. When estimating the costs for *adoption*, we need to exclude any costs for activities that are not related to adoption. Our broad-brush approach in this stage of the research was to use the data on proportion of time spent on adoption activities to adjust the team's costs. Thus, where a team was reported to spend only 90 per cent of their time on adoption activities, only 90 per cent of their staff-related costs would be included in our estimates. It is these adjusted costs that are reported as salary-related costs in Table 11.5.

Table 11.5 also shows the level of expenditure reported by agencies on

*Table 11.5*
**Costs of annual salaries and other selected items**

| | LAs | | | VAAs | | |
|---|---|---|---|---|---|---|
| *Component*[1] | *Mean £000s* | *Range £000s* | *No. agencies* | *Mean £000s* | *Range £000s* | *No. agencies* |
| Salary costs[2] | £402.5 | £86.5–£1574.4 | 27 | £419.3 | £94.8–£1246.6 | 10 |
| Adoption panel | £20.0 | £0.5–£82.9 | 25 | £6.6 | £0–£17.0 | 7 |
| Inter-agency fees | £122.1 | £0–£406.6 | 26 | – | – | – |
| Consortium fees | £13.4 | £0–£86.1 | 24 | £0.4 | £0–£1.0 | 4 |
| Service Level Agreements | £14.1 | £0–£56.0 | 23 | – | – | – |
| Preparation of profiles aided by external organisation | – | £0–£0.2 | 18[3] | – | – | – |
| Subcontracting adoption support services | £10.2 | £0–£45.0 | 19 | – | – | – |
| Other budget items[2] | £470.1 | £-4.0–1761.3[4] | 27 | £138.1 | £5.9–£516.2 | 10 |
| **Total budget**[2] | **£1011.6** | **£100.0–£3595.8** | **27**[5] | **£562.2** | **£106.2–£1762.8** | **10**[5] |

*Notes:*

[1] Not all budget items were reported separately.

[2] These figures have been adjusted for the proportion of time the team spends on adoption activities.

[3] 17 agencies reported £0 for this item.

[4] For one local authority the budget items reportedly separately added to more than the total stated budget.

[5] Number of teams reporting the total budget figure, although data on the separate components are not available for all of these teams.

items commissioned from outside the agency. These items were selected as those that are central to the organisation of adoption services today and for which it was felt answers would be relatively easy to find: i.e. panel arrangements, payment to external agencies to prepare children's profiles, subcontracting adoption support services, inter-agency fees, consortium fees and Service Level Agreements. Average and range of spend on these items are reported in Table 11.5 alongside the number of teams reporting each item.

With the exception of salary-related costs, it is generally local authorities that reported expenditure in the selected areas, reflecting their wider area of responsibility. As we did not ask for expenditure on all budget items and we report averages across responding local authorities and voluntary agencies in Table 11.5, the figures for the separate items will not add up to the total budget given in the final row.

The difference between mean total budgets for local authorities and voluntary agencies shown in Table 11.5 appears large but it is not statistically significant, although, given the massive variation within the local authority and voluntary agency samples, these are small numbers for cost comparisons. Across all the agencies in the costs sample, adoption staff salaries accounted for 45 per cent of the reported budget. On average, staff salaries absorbed around 40 per cent of the budget in local authority teams and the other identified items (such as the inter-agency fees) absorbed a further 15 per cent. Among the voluntary agencies, staff salaries absorbed 75 per cent of the total reported budget.

The penultimate row of Table 11.5 shows the average cost of the items not reported separately in the survey.[17] For the local authorities, these absorb slightly more of the budget than the salary costs, on average 46 per cent of total costs. The figure for the voluntary agencies is much lower, amounting to only about a third of the salary costs or around 24 per cent of the total budget. We cannot identify what any of the agencies have included in this "other budget items" figure, but it might include some

---

[17] Calculated as the total adjusted budget less adjusted salary costs less the costs for the specified items.

salary-related costs, staff travel, office expenses, expenses paid to birth and (potential) adopting parents, costs associated with maintaining the premises or training, and various support costs and overheads. For the local authorities, it may also include adoption allowances.

## Unit costs for some adoption activities

We were able to calculate four output-based unit costs[18] based on the hours local authorities and voluntary agencies reported they spent on each process. These were:

- cost per child assessment;
- cost per adopter assessment;
- cost per child profiled;
- cost of talking to other workers, children and prospective families as part of the linking process.

As discussed earlier, we asked the adoption agencies to report how many hours it took to complete the last child assessment, adopter assessment, etc. This was multiplied by the cost per staff hour for that team, which was estimated using the number of fte staff in each team and the total adoption-related costs for each team, excluding the costs of the specific items (such as inter-agency fees) identified in Table 11.5. Average costs per hour were £35.50 across the 36 adoption agencies. At £40.46 (sd 24.4), the cost per team hour was higher in local authorities than in voluntary agencies (£24.17, sd 7.8) and this difference was statistically significant (p = 0.005). Again, the data do not allow us to explain this difference, but it could be due to a range of factors, including those related

---

[18] Outputs can be thought of as what is "produced". A factory gives a much simplified analogy. Outputs from a car factory might be measured as the number of car radiators or headlight units made. A more global output measure would be the number of complete cars produced, yet the cars cannot be completed without the radiators or headlights. Similarly, each of the four activities identified in the main text are processes that must occur in order to achieve a "child placed for adoption", the main output measure used by central government as a performance indicator for adoption.

to staff costs (higher salaries perhaps) or less direct factors such as the scope of costs included in the "other budget items" figure. However, here our interest is not in these costs per hour *per se* but in using these data to calculate a unit cost for each of the processes. To help understand the range of costs we expected to find, we also asked agencies to report whether the last case had been particularly complex and the period of time over which the process had occurred.

## Cost per child assessment

We were able to calculate the costs of assessing a child for 14 adoption agencies, all of which were local authorities. The mean cost of assessing a child across these agencies was £2,513, although the median was much lower (£1,478), indicating that a few high-cost assessments pulled the mean upwards. The range was wide, between £150 and £9,710. When the two higher-cost cases were omitted, the mean was reduced to £1,447 and the median to £1,104; the range was then between £150 and £3,623. However, these higher-cost cases were two of the three which agencies identified as "particularly complex". In five of these agencies, responsibility for the case was transferred to an adoption/permanency team at adoption recommendation or when the placement order was made (see Chapter 4), but the numbers are too small to say with any certainty whether this transfer generated higher or lower costs.

On average, the assessments took 55 hours to complete (range, six to 200 hours) over an average period of 15.5 weeks (range three to 60 weeks). Not surprisingly, the two higher-cost cases came at the top end of both these ranges.

## Cost per adopter assessment

We were able to calculate the costs of assessing prospective adopters using the Prospective Adopter's Report (or Form F) for 33 agencies: 22 local authorities and 11 voluntary agencies. The mean cost was £2,181 with a lower median at £1,601. The range of costs was wide (£128 and £7,266) with the highest cost more than 1.5 times the second highest. When the highest-cost assessment was excluded, the mean costs were closer to the median at £2,022 and £1,597 respectively. The highest-cost case took 130 hours to complete, but the local authority reported that it was not a particularly complex case. There was no difference in these unit costs between local authorities and voluntary agencies, whether the highest-cost case was included or excluded.

These adopter assessments took an average of 64 hours to complete (median, 60 hours) with the shortest taking 16 hours and the longest taking 170 hours – over 1.5 times the next longest assessment. The mean period over which it was completed was 25 weeks (median, 24) within a range of ten to 99 weeks.

Four agencies thought their last assessment was particularly complex and four did not; 18 did not answer this question.

## Cost per child profiled

We were able to calculate the costs of preparing a child's profile for 22 agencies, all of which were local authorities and none of which reported using an outside organisation to assist in the development of a child's profile (data missing for two cases). The mean cost of time taken by workers to profile a child was £245. The range was wide, with three cases (all from local authorities) costing more than £700, at least twice as much as the next closest cost. The only two cases reported as being particularly complex were among these higher-cost cases. Without these three cases, the mean cost comes down to £147 and the median is closer at £132.

On average, the profile took just under six hours to complete (median, four hours) although the range was wide – from one to 18 hours.

## Cost of talking to children and families as part of the linking process

We were able to calculate some of the costs involved in linking a child to prospective adopters for 12 agencies; again, all were in the local authority sector. We asked how much time was spent talking to prospective families, children and the professionals involved in the case. The mean cost for this work was £1,167 but the median was much lower at £443. The highest cost for this activity was more than four times as much as the next costly example and took a total of 163 hours – more than five times the length of the second-longest time estimate – and was considered to be a particularly complex case. Excluding this higher-cost case brought the mean and median closer at £615 and £405 respectively.

Talking to children and families as part of the linking and matching process took an average of 28.5 hours, coming down to 16 (median 15) when the highest-cost case was removed. Even so, there was a six-fold difference in the range of hours absorbed: from five to 30. Just five agencies felt the case to which the time estimates relate was particularly complex and for each of these the costs were in the higher range.

These agencies were fairly (nine) and very (three) prepared to incur additional costs in their search strategies for children. Eleven agencies sometimes spot-purchased inter-agency placements and one rarely did so. Only three agencies had any restrictions on the number of inter-agency placements that could be made and only one had a potential link stopped in the previous year because of budget restrictions.

## Time spent on linking and matching activities

When asking how much staff time was allocated to adoption activities, we also posed two further questions that were designed to elicit data on the amount of adoption-related time spent on linking and matching activities. On the advice of our advisory group, the questions related to two distinct parts of the work of adoption agencies: linking and matching children within their agencies to any prospective adopters, and linking adopters they had approved to children from outside their agency. Tables 11.6 and 11.7 summarise these data for our costs sample, for those agencies that

*Table 11.6*
**Proportion of adoption-related time spent on linking and matching children in their agency to any prospective adopters**

| % adoption time | Number of agencies | | |
| | With cost data | Without cost data | All agencies |
|---|---|---|---|
| None | 6 | 2 | 8 |
| 2%–10% | 1 | 1 | 2 |
| 20%–30% | 12 (36%) | 7 (30%) | 19 (34%) |
| 33%–50% | 11 (33%) | 8 (35%) | 19 (34%) |
| 60% | 2 | 3 | 5 |
| 70%–75% | 1 | 2 | 3 |
| No. agencies with data | 33/41 | 23/48 | 56/89 |

*Table 11.7*

**Proportion of adoption-related time spent on linking and matching prospective adopters they approved to children from outside their agency**

| % adoption time | Number of agencies | | |
| --- | --- | --- | --- |
| | With cost data | Without cost data | All agencies |
| 2%–10% | 12 (33%) | 7 (26%) | 19 (30%) |
| 12%–20% | 9 (25%) | 8 (29%) | 17 (27%) |
| 25%–30% | 10 (28%) | 7 (26%) | 17 (27%) |
| 33%–40% | 3 | 2 | 5 |
| 42%–50% | 2 | 1 | 3 |
| 100% | 0 | 2 | 2 |
| No. agencies with data 36/41 | | 27/48 | 63/89 |

did not provide sufficient cost-related data, and for the full sample of survey respondents.

Again, we can see that our sample is reasonably representative. Two-thirds of each sample spent between a fifth and a half of their adoption-related time on linking and matching children to any prospective adopters. More than 80 per cent of each sample reported spending less than a third of their time on linking and matching their own adopters to children from outside their agency. Only two agencies reported that they spent 100 per cent of their time on this last task, neither of which provided cost-related data.

## Summary: the costs of adoption activities

It is important to remember that we present these data on the costs of adoption activities with several notes of caution. In the first place, our sample of 41 "costed" adoption agencies is quite small, both in terms of the total number of adoption agencies in England and Wales (a total of just over 200) and in terms of the wide cost variations generated. Second, a postal or web-based survey has limitations (see Chapter 2) and there were insufficient resources within the research budget to be able to confirm the data sent or collect new data.

We have counteracted these limitations as much as possible. For

149

example, our analysis has shown that along many dimensions the "costs sample" is representative of a wider set of agencies, although of course, the extent to which this is also true of their funding or expenditure patterns cannot be judged. We also carefully explored the data sent to us by the adoption agencies to check whether the service description and expenditure data were broadly consistent both within and between teams. Finally, when presenting the costs and unit costs data, we have recorded the details about average measures and ranges alongside information on time spent on the various tasks.

However, costs data in almost any field of social child care are few and far between. While it is important to remember that the unit costs estimated here may not be perfect and certainly should not be used unthinkingly, it is also important that our findings encourage other researchers, practitioners and managers to think more carefully about their costs and processes.

There is no doubt that the processes undertaken to place a child for adoption are time consuming. On average, each child assessment takes 55 hours to complete over a four-month period at a cost of £2,500. Although completing the assessment form for prospective adoptive families absorbed slightly more social work time (64 hours), the average cost was slightly lower at £2,200 and took place over about six months. Talking to children, families and professionals as part of the linking process absorbed a further 3.5 days at a total of £1,200. In this part of the study, the data do not allow us to identify the reasons for the considerable varia-tion around these averages, although there is some evidence to suggest that costs were higher where agencies identified the case as particularly complex. Some of the variation may also be due to differences in the scope of the expenditure provided, or the different accounting – or social work – practices in each agency.

We can compare some of these data with earlier work. Following discussions with social workers and team managers in one of two local authorities, Selwyn and colleagues (2006) found that completing a Child's Permanence Report (CPR) took 20 hours, plus two hours for the medical, 25 hours working towards adoption with the birth family, and some support from the manager's office. Selwyn *et al*'s study also found that completing a Form F for an adopter assessment took 60 hours[19] and talking to children and families absorbed 29 hours. Thus, both Selwyn's study and our study report broadly similar amounts of time for activities, despite the use of very different methodologies.

In this study, we have estimated the costs of four adoption activities, each of which is part of the process of linking and matching children with prospective adoptive families. Of course, many other activities are under-taken as part of the adoption process, including completing the various legal procedures, writing reports for adoption panel meetings, and preparing and introducing children and adoptive families. Each of these activities will involve considerable amounts of social work time and input from other professionals, thereby adding to the costs shown here. Indeed, across the local authorities and voluntary adoption agencies providing sufficient data for this study, the average cost for the four processes amount to just over £6,100, yet this is only about half the cost of adoption estimated in the study of non-infant adoptions referred to above (£14,700 at current prices;[20] Selwyn *et al*, 2006) which included a wider range of adoption activities.

---

[19] When the time taken for preparatory group work, visiting referees and other linked tasks were included, Selwyn *et al* estimated a total of 94 hours.

[20] Adjusted to current prices using the Personal Social Services pay and prices index (Curtis and Netten, 2006).

# 12 Summary and conclusions

This report has focused on findings from a self-completion survey of linking and matching practice in adoption agencies in England and Wales. The questionnaires were primarily completed by adoption service managers in local authority and voluntary adoption agencies.

This area of practice has not previously been investigated systematically. The research was, therefore, intended to be exploratory and the findings are necessarily descriptive. Because this is a new area, there is relatively little comparative research material available but we were able to compare some of our findings with a report on adoption agency inspections by the Commission for Social Care Inspection (CSCI) (2006b).

Although the primary focus was on linking and matching in adoption, it was important to gather a considerable amount of relevant contextual information. Therefore, this report has detailed agency practice in the assessment and preparation of children, recruitment strategies, assessment and preparation of adopters and the operation of the adoption panel, as well as in family finding, linking and matching. As with all self-completion instruments, there were inevitably areas in which the information provided was tantalisingly incomplete.

We begin this chapter by providing a summary and discussion of the findings presented in previous chapters. We conclude by addressing our third and final aim for this survey: to develop a typology of practice in linking and matching.

## The profile of participating agencies

The report has focused on responses from 44 per cent of local authorities and 55 per cent of voluntary adoption agencies in England and Wales. This response rate was broadly in line with other similar surveys. The sample comprised agencies from all regions of the country and all types of councils. As far as we could judge, the local authorities responding to the survey were broadly representative of all agencies in England and

Wales, although there were some indications that responding agencies may have been engaged in a greater volume of adoption work over a longer period.

Analysis of the statistical information provided by agencies suggested that, in relation to the adoption of looked after children, there was considerable variation in the proportion of children adopted by their existing foster carers (from none to over a third of agency placements), whilst placement with single, same-sex or disabled adopters was uniformly rare. There was great variation in the proportion of agencies that were able to place children with their own adopters, from some which placed all their children with adopters recruited by them to a few placing no children in this way. Shire counties, in particular, were more self-sufficient in terms of being able to place children with families recruited by them. This is likely to be due to their geographical size, the greater diversity of residents and multiplicity of population centres. Respondents from many other types of local authority commented that various features to do with their geographic position or local population profile impinged on their ability to place within their own resources. In keeping with this, we found that shire counties recruited markedly more adopters than other local authorities. Interestingly, we also found that, on average, voluntary agencies converted more (50%) enquiries into approved adopters than did local authorities (25%).

Agency statistics showed that, on average, just over half the placements made were in-house, placements made through consortia arrangements accounted for just over a quarter and other inter-agency arrangements secured placements for the remainder. Overall, the proportion of placements achieved through a link from the Adoption Register was relatively small, but this was an important source for some agencies. On average, agencies reported inter-agency fees being payable for around 35 or 40 per cent of cases. There were indications that voluntary agencies were used less readily than other local authorities. This is consistent with comments from voluntary agency respondents in the current study and with the recent report by Deloitte on the commissioning of voluntary agency placements (Deloitte, 2006).

It was also interesting to find that the proportion of children placed with a sibling varied from 14 to 80 per cent of placed children. Such a spread might indicate differential policies on the separation of sibling groups or indeed on the timing of taking children into care and moving them on to adoption, leading to varying numbers of sibling groups referred for adoption, an issue to which we return in the second stage of this study. Similarly, the proportion of placed children who had special health needs or disabilities was reported as varying from none to 29 per cent. While there may be some variation in what is considered a "disability", this finding might indicate greater determination to place such children for adoption in some agencies than in others.

## The assessment and preparation of children

The survey showed variation in the assessment and preparation of children, particularly in relation to the extent and timing of the transfer of case responsibility from one section of service to another and the level of involvement of adoption/permanence specialists in case management. Where case responsibility transferred completely, it generally did so at around the time that a placement order was granted. Thus, the Child's Permanence Report (CPR) would be prepared by one worker and another would take over to complete preparatory work and placement tasks. Some respondents to the survey found this practice unhelpful in that the new worker often lacked an in-depth knowledge of the child and his or her history and needs. However, others argue that case management by specialist adoption teams reduces delays for children because of the level of expertise of the workers involved. There is undoubtedly a tension here and one that could fruitfully be further explored – and, indeed, this issue will be further examined in the second stage of this study.

Little was revealed from the survey about the use of any particular structured approaches to assist in the *assessment* of children for adoption. In terms of developments in this area of work, sibling assessment was frequently cited and several agencies mentioned joint working with, or opportunities to refer to, mental health specialists where necessary. Twelve agencies had consultancy arrangements in place to aid social workers and others in their assessment work with children (for example, from a clinical psychologist or multi-agency team); in seven of these agencies, psychologists were attached to the adoption team. Eight agencies particularly emphasised assessments of the child's attachment status and two used Story Stem narratives as part of assessing children's needs.

Direct work to prepare children for permanence is the responsibility of the child's allocated social worker and, according to Romaine and her colleagues (2007), this is the person who should undertake the work in the majority of cases. However, in the responses to our question about practice development in this area, the thrust seemed to be towards introducing another worker to undertake the task. Agencies that delegated this role tended to take one of two major approaches: one was to refer to a specialist worker (29 agencies) and the other was to engage social work assistants. The rationale for introducing another practitioner to do this work may be based on the belief that this other worker will be more able to focus their attention on the child without the distraction of emergency work that so often afflicts children's social workers. According to a recent report by the CSCI (2006b), 'in a fifth of agencies children's social workers struggled to prioritise this essential work, leaving some children in a very vulnerable situation'. It seems to us that there is no reason why unqualified workers should not possess the qualities needed for direct work, but there is a question about the level of training and supervision that might be available to them. We are unable to add further to this debate from this study but this is an area that might provide useful information if tackled as a specific issue.

The question of placing siblings together or apart arose frequently in the course of looking at children's assessments and, as we have seen, there was variation between agencies in the proportion of children placed with a sibling. Rushton (2000) identified this area as one of the ongoing dilemmas in adoption practice and it seems that it continues to exercise the practice field. Although there is some research and practice evidence on siblings in an adoption context (see, for example, Rushton et al, 2001), no study has yet been able to provide robust evidence on which to base decisions and there are obvious difficulties in placing some sibling groups if, for example, the group is large in number, there are large age gaps or high levels of individual need. There are a variety of factors that might account for the variation in the frequency of sibling group placement across agencies. It might be that some agencies move more quickly in terms of taking children into care and moving them on to permanence by adoption. This could imply that siblings are placed sequentially and, perhaps, separately. Other agencies might focus on family support for much longer, resulting in brothers and sisters becoming looked after at the same time. Alternatively, it is likely that some agencies have a policy of not separating children even when it would expedite placements, while others prioritise securing placements over the need to keep siblings together. Certainly, there was some variation in whether agencies saw keeping siblings together as essential or merely desirable. Whilst this survey cannot answer these questions, again it highlights an area for future research.

## Recruitment and preparation of adopters

Agencies told us that there continued to be difficulty in recruiting sufficient adopters for children with additional needs, particularly families able to consider children with disabilities, those with black or minority ethnic backgrounds and, to some extent, for older children and those with special health needs. Perhaps surprisingly, about a quarter of the agencies did not appear to operate targeted recruitment drives to find families able to meet such needs. This is consistent with findings from adoption agencies' inspections (CSCI, 2006b), where three out of ten local authorities and one out of ten voluntary agencies had not developed strategies to recruit adoptive parents to meet the needs of children who were waiting.

In terms of special tools and practice approaches for working with prospective adopters, we noted that more voluntary agencies offered examples of practice than did local authorities, although we cannot be sure if this was an indication of greater innovation or if voluntary agencies were more likely to take the opportunity to describe their practice.

The most commonly mentioned tools in this section of the survey were attachment style or status assessments that were incorporated, in full or in part, into the home study phase of adopter assessment by 14 per cent of agencies.[21] The other notable development was in the area of mentoring and support for prospective adopters in the preparatory phase by more experienced adopters and the use of support groups. There was also mention of the use of a focused training day for new adoptive parents and their support network in order to discuss the specific needs of the child to be placed.

## Linking children and families: profiling and family finding

In the majority of cases, children's profiles seem to be quite simple and brief. It is likely that, for many children who are matched in-house, a profile is never needed. Several agencies mentioned using profiles only for some children, presumably those they anticipate being more difficult to place and whose particular needs might be met only through searching further afield. In general, where profiling was required, this was the responsibility of the family-finding worker. Although family-finding workers may have less knowledge of the children than children's social workers, they will have more familiarity with the linking mechanisms available and with the style and formats required for different media. Cousins (2005) has noted the skills needed to write an effective profile and this was borne out in Selwyn and colleagues' (2008) finding that the profiles of black and minority ethnic children were sometimes poorly written and often stressed the complexity of a child's ethnicity and asked for an adoptive family that could meet all the child's cultural and identity needs.

In the majority of agencies, the family-finding worker would meet with the child before embarking on the linking task. However, in 14 per cent of the responding agencies, the child was rarely or never seen by the

---

[21] The assessment of prospective adoptive families usually incorporates two distinct elements. One part entails group preparation sessions, which require applicants to attend a series of meetings addressing various issues in adoption. The other comprises a series of individual meetings with a social worker. These meetings explore families' strengths and vulnerabilities and provide the material to permit the Prospective Adopter's Report to be completed. This aspect of the process is known as the home study.

family finder. We have been unable to locate any written guidance on whether it is desirable for a family finder to have some direct knowledge of the child. One can see that there might, again, be two equally legitimate points of view. On the one hand, a family finder, who has met the child and carer, will have more first-hand knowledge of the child to convey to prospective families. On the other, if reports are well prepared, it ought to be feasible to make an assessment as to what qualities are required of families from the written material about the child, and introducing another professional to the child might be seen as unnecessary and potentially confusing.

Agencies exploited a variety of mechanisms to locate families for children, but Service Level Agreements were rarely used. From agencies' responses, we identified four different mechanisms for identifying links:

- first-hand knowledge of a potential family assessed by the adoption team;
- links made on paper or by computer (since the establishment of the Adoption Register and some databases run by consortia);
- presentation of a child's profile to the community of approved adopters by, for example, features in the publications *Be My Parent* or *Children Who Wait*, in-house profiling events and exchange events;
- presentation of a child's profile to the wider community through newspapers, radio or television features (rarely used).

The first two of these methods are widely used by all agencies and can be described as "professionally-led" linking, that is, social workers working on behalf of children or families make a professional assessment of the congruence of the characteristics of a child with those of families which may be suitable. The latter two of these methods seek to present inform-ation about children through photos, videos, DVDs and text, and invite people to put themselves forward as potential adoptive parents for the child. The fourth approach is relatively rarely used. However, although these methods are described as "adopter-led", it is still the professionals who ultimately make decisions about which family is most suitable to be matched to the child. It is interesting to note that Selwyn *et al* (2008) found that the likelihood of children being promoted using the latter two approaches was related to agency practice, not to children's needs.

Within each of these categories, a variety of tactics may be used to achieve the desired result, and in recent years there have been significant moves toward further developing adopter-led approaches. This is evidenced by the level of interest in setting up a forum where adopters can view video or DVD footage of children and in the further development of internet sites. Half of the agencies in the survey had secured links through regional adoption events or in-house profiling events, whilst featuring children on the internet had provided some links for 17 per cent of agencies. Specific family-finding magazines such as *Be My Parent* (BAAF) and *Children Who Wait* (Adoption UK) had been used by over 90 per cent of the agencies, although this route accounted for a relatively small proportion of placements made in most agencies.

## The matching process

Two-thirds of the agencies reported that they spent between a fifth and half of their time on linking and matching children to prospective adopters. In terms of the matching process, most agencies (76%) indicated that decisions about which families to proceed with were taken in a formal matching meeting. When formal meetings were not used, children's social workers (sometimes with their managers) would liaise with family-finding workers or adoption team managers in order to reach a decision. In either case, most respondents emphasised that the decision ultimately rested with the children's worker (or their team). It was reported that the child is almost always (98%) asked what the important priorities would be for them in matching, but most agencies (76%) do not involve children in deciding which family to proceed with.

The survey responses did illustrate continuing tensions in relation to how many, and at what stage, families are approached directly to explore whether they might be able to meet a child's needs. Specifically, agencies said they would generally pursue one (13 agencies), two (nine agencies) or more commonly three (25 agencies) links (potential families) at any one time, although a minority reported more. The majority of agencies followed up links primarily through discussions with the workers for the families involved, rather than with the families themselves. Whether the families were made aware that they were being considered for a child varied. It was suggested by some that it could be difficult for prospective adopters when they were made aware of potential links at an early stage because of the anxieties that could be associated with an uncertain outcome and, one assumes, the disappointment that might follow if another family is selected.

A critical part of the linking process is the sharing of information with prospective adoptive families. Ultimately, although social workers may make choices about which families to approach about children, it is the adopters who need to decide whether they wish to care for a particular child. In order to do so, they will need to be aware of all the relevant information concerning the child and his or her experiences to date. All the agencies stated that they used the Child's Permanence Report as a mechanism for presenting information to prospective families, whilst 85 per cent of the agencies shared video images of children. Children's medical and other assessment reports were also made available to adopters by all agencies and were used by about a third of agencies during linking as well as later on.

Children's life story books were also widely used as means of sharing information with adopters, but many agencies (56%) reserved these documents for use after a match had been approved. Sight of the child's case file was available to families in 55 per cent of agencies (although usually reserved until after the matching panel), but almost half of the agencies did not share case files with prospective adopters. Most authorities exploit as many means as possible to ensure that prospective adopters have opportunities to speak to people who know the child from different perspectives, for example, professionals and foster carers, although there was some variation in terms of when these opportunities were made available. Meetings with birth family members almost invariably took place after the match was approved.

Life or Child Appreciation Days (used by about 55% of agencies) were less frequently used than one-to-one contacts, although several agencies did mention that they were interested in (or were in the process of trying to organise) such events. Their use was seen as particularly important for older children or those with more complex histories. For the most part, these events occurred after a match had been approved. "Unseen viewings", where prospective adopters have sight of a child before a match is recommended, without the child knowing who the adopters are, were used by only a minority of agencies (13%), although one agency considered them crucial because they allowed for "emotional chemistry" to enter the equation.

## Priorities and issues in matching

On the basis that it is unlikely that a "perfect" match will be achieved, some element of compromise will often be necessary. In Chapter 1, we discussed the ways in which the matching task has changed in line with the changing profile of children who need adoptive families. In our survey, we used a variety of approaches to explore respondents' views and experiences of the matching process in an attempt to capture not only how the process operated, but also what factors were perceived as facilitating or complicating the task. Beginning with an exploration of respondents' views on the hierarchy of children's needs, we were able to determine that meeting children's emotional, behavioural, attachment and health needs, in concert with the suitability of the adopters' parenting style, were high-priority factors for almost all respondents. Other considerations, including needs in relation to ethnicity or contact, were a lesser priority for some but still very important to the majority (60–70%) of respondents. Ensuring that children's wishes were taken into account was a high priority for about 40 per cent of respondents, but only about one-quarter described matching to keep siblings together or to reflect children's interests or talents as essential elements and, for the great majority of respondents, the wishes of the birth family came lower down the priority list.

In a more open question, we asked respondents to reflect on factors that made for a good match and factors that should preclude a match. Respondents mentioned issues of practice and process within agencies, factors to do with the wider organisation of the agency, consideration of adopters' characteristics, attitudes and understanding of the adoptive parenting task, and finally, consideration of "chemistry" (Schofield et al, 2000; Sinclair and Wilson, 2003). The analysis of these responses showed that matching is about balancing relative strengths and vulnerabilities and that the wider context is important, that is, the way in which an agency operates and the experience and knowledge of the workers directly involved. However, the factor that was mentioned most often, by far, in this context was the importance of having clear and accurate information about both the child and the prospective adopters. This, again, is in line with findings from adoption agency inspections, which have shown that one in six agencies did not get basic factual information correct in children's assessment reports: 'In over half of all agencies, the quality of these reports was described as poor or not of a consistently good quality' (CSCI, 2006b, section 5.11, p16). Similarly, only a third of local authorities' and half of voluntary agencies' Prospective Adopter's Reports were deemed satisfactory by inspectors. One interesting feature from our survey was that few respondents, when asked to identify key factors in matching, specifically mentioned the importance of understanding the child's wishes or expectations.

In looking at barriers to matching, one of the primary problems that respondents identified related to an issue that we touched on in Chapter 1, where we discussed the potential role of professionals' values and beliefs (Gerstenzang and Freundlich, 2006; see also Selwyn et al, 2008). Respondents were concerned here about problems that resulted from the attitudes of some children's social workers who kept looking for the "ideal family" and refused apparently suitable matches. The comments made by respondents in this context were often to do with a reluctance to consider non-traditional family types (single parents or same-sex couples, for example). A related issue, highlighted by responses elsewhere in the questionnaire, was the importance of the child's social worker knowing the child well and the accompanying difficulties when workers changed. The problematic rate of turnover among children's social workers is well known (Local Government Association, 2009). Selwyn et al's study (2008) showed that more than a third of children's social workers had met the child less than four weeks before the research interviews. Moreover, most of the children's social workers in their study had little knowledge about the adoption process. Taken together, these concerns about beliefs and values, coupled with a relatively low probability that the child's worker will know the child's case well, raise the question of the appropriateness of the role of the children's social worker as the final decision maker, which, as mentioned above, was the case in most agencies. Cousins (2008), in a discussion of related issues, comments that making the decision about which family to select is a big responsibility and that a 'wider range of views should be canvassed'.

Other factors that were felt to add to the complexity of the matching task were difficulties in relation to the placement of siblings, contact plans, and complications encountered in adequately reflecting children's ethnic heritage in a proposed adoptive placement (see also Selwyn *et al*, 2008).

One further concern, raised particularly by voluntary agencies, was finance. Several respondents felt that the inter-agency fee was frequently an obstacle to effective matching, particularly as the fee for a family approved by a voluntary agency is considerably higher than that for a family approved by another local authority. Local authority respondents did indeed talk of the need to be prudent with budgets but relatively few agencies reported that a potential match had actually been prevented because of budget issues. Nonetheless, 10 per cent of agencies reported a reluctance to spend money and eight agencies mentioned restrictions on the number of inter-agency placements that could be purchased. It appears that local authorities often proceed sequentially in their search for links, beginning with their own resources, proceeding to use families from their agency consortium if necessary, and only involving other agencies if they have no success with their own or local resources. This approach has particular implications for voluntary adoption agencies, which are reliant on local authorities purchasing placements (see also Deloitte, 2006). It is not possible to say from this survey whether such a sequential approach may lead to delays in finding families for children in individual cases, although a recent study has found such an association (Selwyn *et al*, 2008). This study also showed a surprisingly low use of voluntary agencies to secure placements for black and minority ethnic children, which was the focus of that study, even though most specialise in finding placements for such children, or those with complex needs. In addition, another study by Selwyn and colleagues (2009) suggests that anxieties about the cost of inter-agency placements may be misplaced, because when local authorities are considering these fees they are rarely able to take into account the true costs of in-house placements, which are themselves substantial – especially when placing children with additional needs. Indeed, as previously mentioned, when all such costs are considered, it was found that inter-agency fees represent good value for money.

This exploration of adoption professionals' views on matching issues also showed that there are contrasting views in the field on a number of contentious issues. These include varied opinions on:

- the balance to be struck between matching on ethnicity and avoiding delay;
- how far contact plans should be shaped by what adopters think they can manage;
- how soon the matching criteria (or placement plan) need to be reviewed if no match has been found for a child;
- whether adopter-led matches lead to better outcomes than those that are led by professionals.

## Developments in the matching process

One of the survey respondents commented that matching as a task is, as yet, 'relatively unexplored and conceptually underdeveloped'. In line with this, there appeared to be fewer developments in the matching process than in other aspects of adoption work in many agencies. There were, however, definite signs that some agencies were trying to make the matching process more systematic, by using a matrix or grid to compare children's and families' characteristics (four or five agencies) and to do this more objectively by considering potential links in a formal meeting.

## The adoption panel

Some adoption panels considered all types of permanence decisions while others focused on adoption only. Voluntary agencies, of course, considered only the approval of adopters. On the whole, respondents felt that the move to an independent Chair of the panel had been positive, although several stressed that the quality of chairing depended on the individual Chair and his or her abilities rather than independence *per se*. There was substantial variation between agencies in the frequency with which panels might request further information (for adoption plan recommendations, this varied from none to 30% of cases) or refuse to make a particular recommendation (such as for an adoption recommend-ation, where it varied from none to 18% of cases, or for matching, where it varied from none to 10% of cases). In some agencies this never occurred. Panels that considered a higher number of cases were more likely than others to return papers with requests for further information. This might indicate that the more experienced panels have the confidence to insist on receiving paperwork of a high enough quality for good decision making.

Examples of practice development in terms of working with the panel included the use of checklists and practice guidance tools to assist panel members in making their decisions, joint training for panel members with social workers, and panel members attending external courses. Some agencies spoke of compiling information packs for individuals attending panel. There was also mention of the use of feedback systems to panels from social workers, adopters and, sometimes, children. Several agencies wrote of the involvement of prospective adopters, although prospective adopters must now be invited to attend the panel (Adoption Agencies Regulations, reg. 26(4)), and one or two mentioned that birth parents, or children when old enough, were encouraged to attend the panel when the plan for adoption was being considered. In addition, one agency expected panel members to come to meetings with prepared written comments on the cases under consideration. There was also mention of appraisals for panel members, debriefing after meetings, and a support network for panel members.

## Estimated costs of adoption activities

One very important area in the survey was an investigation of the costs of adoption activities. Because this comprised only a part of the survey, the amount of information that could be requested was limited. There was also much missing data in this section, which meant that a number of questionnaires were not usable for the costs analyses. The sub-sample for which costs were available was, however, broadly representative of adoption agencies in England and Wales.

Despite these limitations, it was possible to estimate costs for adoption teams and calculate costs for four major aspects of adoption work: assessment of children; assessment of adopters; profiling; and the family-finding or linking process. There is no doubt that the processes undertaken to place a child for adoption are time consuming, and rightly so, given the impact such a placement will have on a child's life. On average, each child assessment takes 55 hours to complete over a four-month period at a cost of £2,500. Although completing the assessment form for prospective adoptive families absorbed slightly more social work time (64 hours), the average cost was slightly lower at £2,200, and took place over about six months. Preparing a child's profile (excluding the three highest-costing cases) cost an average of £147 and took six hours to complete. Talking to children, families and professionals as part of the linking process absorbed a further 3.5 days at a total of £1,200.

The number of hours spent on each of these activities was broadly in line with other research (Selwyn et al, 2006) and the average cost of the four processes amounts to over £6,100. These costs reflect the consider-able amount of work devoted to these processes, and it must be recognised that these costs are associated with four discrete activities and should not be considered indicative of the totality of the work involved.

## Developing a typology of practice approaches

One of the purposes of the survey was to try to identify distinctive variations in adoption practice that might lend themselves to further investigation in terms of their effectiveness and their associated costs.

As the analysis of the survey data progressed, it became clear that there were four identifiable practice variations that were likely to be amenable to grouping for the purposes of a comparative study. Other variations could have been included but larger numbers of groups make it difficult to detect statistically significant differences without very large samples. It was also important that the practices selected were embedded as part of an agency's routine practice rather than innovative techniques applicable only to particular cases, as in, for example, referral to specialists for assessment of children's needs. Eventually, we settled on the following four variations in approach, which seem to offer distinctively different ways of managing the adoption process. All of these variations in practice can be seen as ways of trying to improve the effectiveness of either family finding or matching.

1) *The stage at which transfer of case responsibility to adoption and permanence specialists takes place*
As highlighted in Chapter 4, the practice of making an early transfer of case responsibility to adoption specialists is somewhat contentious, with obvious advantages and disadvantages. The arguments for it are that the child is better served by workers with time, a relatively predictable work-load, experience and expertise. On the other hand, the child experiences yet more changes in the people involved with their case, and new workers know less about the child and have to build a rapport rapidly in order to develop a relationship with him or her. It seems important to learn whether or not this practice is associated with a better understanding of the child's needs and a more effective match and whether it brings with it higher or lower costs.

2) *Utilisation of the Attachment Style Interview (ASI)/Adult Attachment Interview (AAI) frameworks in the assessment of adoptive parents*
For some years, research in the child placement field has sought to identify and measure the parenting characteristics of adoptive parents and relate these to adoption outcomes. Although the literature on parenting style and strategy is vast, in recent years the attachment theory framework has been steadily gaining ground in the child development literature generally and in relation to looked after children specifically. The application of the theory to adults as a way of explaining the ways in which they interact and interpret their relationships with others (including their children) is relatively more recent, but has caught the imagination of many child welfare practitioners. Work undertaken relatively recently in the UK (Henderson *et al*, 2003) has suggested that adopters' attachment styles may be associated with children's progress in adoptive placements.

Specifically, these authors have reported a possible association between aggressiveness shown by children in their completion of Story Stems some time after placement and adoptive parents who have an insecure or unresolved attachment status. However, it is important to note that great care is needed in interpreting and applying the results of the AAI. In reviewing the literature on this topic, Aldgate and Jones (2005) suggest that:

> ... *in assessing foster and adoptive parents, the sense they have made of their attachment experiences* **may** *be a contributing factor to their responses and coping mechanisms in relation to the children in their care.* (p 90, emphasis added)

If the AAI and ASI are indeed able to guide practitioners as to where support may be needed, then matches made with the benefit of this additional information might be expected to be more effective. However, the AAI procedure requires a trained interviewer and someone trained to reliably code the interview. Thus, if used routinely within an agency, it would also be expected to increase costs substantially, at least in the short term in relation to training in the use of the instruments and in interpreting the results.

**3) *Adopter-led methods using profiling events: that is, where a variety of media are used to profile children needing adoption directly to prospective adopters (for example, using written profiles, children's artwork, photographs, DVDs, etc)***

As previously mentioned, profiling children directly to prospective adoptive families is a fairly recent development in the family-finding or linking process in this country. Proponents emphasise that by presenting meaningful visual and audio images of real children, prospective adopters are more able to make an informed assessment of whether they might be able to parent a child. It also allows prospective adopters to be proactive in seeking a child or children to adopt and to identify a child with whom they feel some "chemistry". The method lends itself particularly to situations in which children's characteristics presented on paper might suggest a more complex parenting task. It is easy to see that such images of children might appear quite compelling to adoptive families and encourage them to make a degree of emotional commitment to the child. However, others see that very commitment as potentially dangerous, in that it might encourage families to proceed without paying sufficient attention to aspects of a child's needs that they might find more difficult to meet or deal with. Because this approach is relatively new but rapidly gaining ground with the advent of internet family-finding sites and the increasing interest in profiling events, it seemed apposite to include this as one of the major practice approaches.

### 4) *The routine use of matching tools and formalised meetings*

This is our final category of practice and the only one that focuses specifically on matching. This is indicative of the relative lack of practice development in this area to date. The use of tools such as grids or matrices to aid the matching task might be expected to ensure a more thorough and systematic approach by detailing the needs of a child and how each of the families being considered might be able to meet those needs. Formalising the decision-making through the use of meetings (sometimes accompanied by set timescales) might also be expected to remove some of the subjectivity from the decision-making process and the burden of responsibility from one individual social worker. Whether these processes do enhance the decision-making process and whether there are significant additional costs needs to be explored.

## Conclusion

Overall, the survey reveals that there is significant variation in adoption practice across agencies and also much innovation in practice, although relatively little of it is at present directed at matching. The report provides costings for four areas of adoption activity and highlights a number of novel ideas and developments; although very few have been subject to any evaluation, they may be of interest to policy makers and practitioners. We have identified a number of issues that were seen by respondents as obstacles to making timely adoption placements as well as areas where there are diametrically opposed views amongst practitioners on key aspects of the adoption process. Some of these issues are in need of

169

further research, while others will be addressed by the second stage of this research.

Of particular importance is the need for further work to understand why there might be such a large variation between local authorities in the proportion of children who are placed with their siblings and what might be the longer-term implications of these decisions for adopted children. The same is true for disability – it seems crucial to learn whether there are any real differences in the way that different local authorities plan for the long-term care of children with a disability or serious health condition.

While it would not be appropriate to draw implications for policy or practice from this kind of survey, the results do provide an interesting snapshot of current practice in England and Wales and guidance on where attention might usefully be focused in future research.

# References

Adoption Agencies Regulations (2005) Statutory Instrument No. 389, section 17, paragraph 1, London: HMSO

Adoption Register for England and Wales (2007) *Annual Report* [online]. Available at: www.adoptionregister.org.uk/files/annualreport07.pdf [accessed 6 September 2009]

Aldgate J. and Jones D. (2005) 'The place of attachment in children's development', in Aldgate J., Jones D., Rose W. and Jeffrey C., *The Developing World of the Child*, London: Jessica Kingsley Publishers

Archer C. and Gordon C. (2004) 'Parent mentoring: an innovative approach to adoption support', *Adoption & Fostering*, 28:4, pp 27–38

Avery R (1999) *New York State's Longest Waiting Children 1998: A study of New York state children in need of adoptive families*, Ithaca, NY: Cornell University. Available at: www.nysccc.org/longestwaiting.pdf

BAAF (1998) *Key Issues in Assessment*, London: BAAF

BAAF (2005a) *Finding Families for Children via the Internet (FF4C): Report on the survey of local authority adoption agencies* [online]. Available at: www.baaf.org.uk/res/pubs/books/la_rpt.pdf

BAAF (2005b) *Finding Families for Children via the Internet (FF4C): Voluntary adoption agencies survey report* [online]. Available at: www.baaf.org.uk/res/pubs/books/vaa_rpt.pdf

BAAF (2005c) *Finding Families for Children via the Internet (FF4C): Independent foster care providers' survey report* [online]. Available at: www.baaf.org.uk/res/pubs/books/ifp.pdf

BAAF (2006) *Inter-Agency Fees 1 April 2006–31 March 2007* [online]. Available at: www.baaf.org.uk/info/financial/iafees2006.pdf [accessed 20 August 2007]

Barnett D. and Moroney C. (2004) *Survey of Existing Child Profiling Websites in the UK and North America*, Part of the Finding Families for Children via the Internet Project, London: BAAF

Barth R. and Berry M. (1988) *Adoption and Disruption: Rates, risks and responses*, New York: Aldine de Gruyter

Beecham J. (2000) *Unit Costs: Not exactly child's play*, Joint publication from the Department of Health, Personal Social Services Research Unit and Dartington Social Care Research Unit, London: Department of Health

Beecham J., Chisholm D., O'Herlihy A. and Astin J. (2003) 'Variations in the costs of child and adolescent psychiatric inpatient units', *British Journal of Psychiatry*, 183, pp 220–225

Beecham J., Greco V., Sloper P. and Webb R. (2007) 'The costs of key worker support for disabled children and their families', *Child: Care, Health & Development*, 33:5, pp 611–618

Bifulco A. (2006) *Summary Interpretation of ASI-AF: Some indications on how to interpret the ASI-AF in adoption and fostering assessments* [online]. Available at: www.attachmentstyleinterview.com/pdf%20files/ASI_AFsumInterpret.pdf [accessed September 2009]

Bifulco A., Lillie A., Ball B. and Moran P. (1998) *Attachment Style Interview (ASI): Training manual*, London: Royal Holloway, University of London

Blatchford P., Bassett P., Brown P., Martin C., Russell A., Webster R. and Haywood N. (2006) *The Deployment and Impact of Support Staff in Schools: Findings from a national questionnaire survey of schools, support staff and teachers*, London: Department for Education and Skills

Borland M., O'Hara G. and Triseliotis J. (1991) 'Placement outcomes for children with special needs', *Adoption & Fostering*, 75:2, pp 18–28

Bretherton I., Ridgeway D. and Cassidy J. (1990) 'Assessing internal working models of the attachment relationship: an attachment story completion task for three-year-olds', in Greenberg M. T., Cicchetti D. and Cummings E. M. (eds) *Attachment in the Preschool Years*, London: University of Chicago Press, pp 273–308

Commission for Social Care Inspection (CSCI) (2006a) *Social Services Performance Assessment Framework Indicators (Children)* [online]. Available at: www.ofsted.gov.uk/Ofsted-home/Publications-and-research/Browse-all-by/Documents-by-type/Statistics/Performance-assessment-framework-indicators-PAF-reports-and-data [accessed September 2009], p 58

Commission for Social Care Inspection (2006b) *Adoption: Messages from inspections of adoption agencies*, London: Commission for Social Care Inspection

Cousins J. (2003) 'Are we missing the match? Re-thinking adopter assessment and child profiling', *Adoption & Fostering*, 27:4, pp 7–17

Cousins J. (2005) 'Disabled children who need permanence: barriers to placement', *Adoption & Fostering*, 29:3, pp 6–20

Cousins J. (2008) *Ten Top Tips for Finding Families for Children*, London: BAAF

Curtis L. and Netten A. (eds) (2006) *The Unit Costs of Health and Social Care*, Canterbury: PSSRU, University of Kent

Dance C. and Rushton A. (2005) 'Joining a new family: the views and experiences of adopted and fostered young people', *Adoption & Fostering*, 29:2, pp 18–28

Deloitte (2006) *Commissioning Voluntary Sector Adoption Agencies*, London: Department for Education and Skills. Available at: www.dcsf.gov.uk/everychild matters/resources-and-practice/RS00032/

Department for Education and Skills (2003a) *National Minimum Standards: Voluntary adoption agencies and LA adoption service* [online]. Available at: www. everychildmatters.gov.uk/resources-and-practice/ig00026/ [accessed September 2009]

Department for Education and Skills (2003b) *Draft Adoption Regulations and Guidance for Consultation: Arranging adoptions and assessing prospective adopters*, London: Department for Education and Skills

Department for Education and Skills (2005) *Statistical First Release: Survey of children and young people receiving personal social services in England aged 10–17: 2004–2005* [online]. Available at: www.dfes.gov.uk/rsgateway/DB/SFR/ s000622/sfr54-2005.pdf [accessed September 2009]

Department of Health, Department for Education and Employment, Home Office (2000) *Framework for the Assessment of Children in Need and their Families*, London: The Stationery Office

Dyer C. (2002) 'Couple sue over adopted "wild child"', *The Guardian*, 17 October 2002

Evaluation Trust and Hadley Centre for Adoption and Foster Care Studies (2007) *A Summary of the Evaluation of Adoption UK's Parenting Support Programme 'It's a Piece of Cake'* [online]. Available at: www.adoptionuk.com/images/ Cake%20evaluation%20summary%20report.pdf [accessed September 2009]

Evan B. Donaldson Adoption Institute (2004) *What's Working for Children: A policy study of adoption stability and termination*, New York: Evan B Donaldson Adoption Institute

Farnfield S (2008) 'A theoretical model for the comprehensive assessment of parenting', *British Journal of Social Work*, 38, pp 1076–1099

Festinger T. (1990) 'Adoption disruption: rates and correlates', in Brodzinsky D. and Schechter M. (eds) *The Psychology of Adoption*, New York: Oxford University Press, pp 201–218

Festinger T. (2002) 'After adoption: dissolution or permanence?', *Child Welfare*, 81:3, pp 515–33

Frazer L. and Selwyn J. (2005) 'Why are we waiting? The demography of adoption for children of black, Asian and black mixed parentage in England', *Child and Family Social Work*, 10, pp 135–47

Freundlich M., Gerstenzang S. and Holtan M. (2007) 'Websites featuring children waiting for adoption: a cross-country review', *Adoption & Fostering*, 31:2, pp 6–16

George C., Kaplan N. and Main M. (1985) *The Adult Attachment Interview*, unpublished manuscript, Berkeley: University of California at Berkeley, Department of Psychology

Gerstenzang S. and Freundlich M. (2006) *Finding a Fit that will Last a Lifetime: A guide to connecting adoptive families with waiting children*, Answering the Call Series, AdoptUsKids: www.adoptuskids.org

Goodman R. (1997) 'The Strengths and Difficulties Questionnaire: a research note', *Journal of Child Psychology and Psychiatry*, 38, pp 581–86

Grinyer A. (2002) 'The anonymity of research participants: assumptions, ethics and practicalities', *Social Research Update*, 36, pp 1–4

Groze V. (1996) 'A 1 and 2 year follow-up study of adoptive families and special needs children', *Children and Youth Services Review*, 18:1–2, pp 57–82

Hadley Centre for Adoption and Foster Care Studies (2002) *Matching Children and Families in Permanent Placement: A research summary*, Bristol: School for Policy Studies, University of Bristol

Harnott C. and Humphreys H. (2004) *Permanence Planning: Notes for practitioners*, London: Social Care Institute for Excellence

Henderson K., Hillman S., Hodges J., Kaniuk J. and Steele M. (2003) 'Attachment representations and adoption: associations between maternal states of mind and emotion narratives in previously maltreated children', *Journal of Child Psychotherapy*, 29:2, pp 187–205

Hodges J., Steele M., Hillman S., Henderson K. and Kaniuk J. (2003) 'Changes in attachment representations over the first year of adoptive placement: narratives of maltreated children', *Clinical Child Psychology and Psychiatry*, 8:3, pp 351–67

Howe D. (1995) *Attachment Theory for Social Work Practice*, London: MacMillan Press

Ivaldi G. (2000) *Surveying Adoption: A comprehensive analysis of local authority adoption 1998–1999 (England)*, London: BAAF

Local Government Association (2009) *Respect and Protect: Respect, recruitment and retention in children's social work*, London: LGA (3 March 2009)

Local Government Data Unit (Wales) (2007) *Children Looked After by Local Authorities, Year Ending 31 March 2006* [online]. Available at: http://dissemination.dataunitwales.gov.uk/webview/index.jsp [accessed September 2009]

Lord J. (2008) *The Adoption Process in England: A guide for children's social workers*, London: BAAF

Lord J. and Borthwick S. (2008) *Together or Apart? Assessing brothers and sisters for permanent placement*, London: BAAF

Lowe N., Murch M., Borkowski M., Weaver A., Thomas C. and Beckford V. (1999) *Supporting Adoption: Reframing the approach*, London: BAAF

McRoy R. G. (1999) *Special Needs Adoptions: Practice issues*, New York: Garland Publishing Inc

Millard Veevers H. (1991) 'Which child, which family?', *Adoption & Fostering*, 15:1, pp 42–46

Monck E. (2001) 'Concurrent planning in the adoption of children under eight years', *Adoption & Fostering*, 25:1, pp 67–68

Mulcahy J. (2000) *It's a Piece of Cake?*, Banbury, Oxfordshire: Adoption UK

National Foundation for Educational Research (2004) *General Teaching Council Survey of Teachers 2004*, London: General Teaching Council for England. Available at: http://publications.teachernet.gov.uk/eOrderingDownload/teacher survey.pdf [accessed September 2009]

O'Reilly M. (2007) 'Finding families on the web: *Be My Parent* goes online in the UK', *Adoption & Fostering*, 31:2, pp 17–21

Owen M. (1999) *Novices, Old Hands, and Professionals: Adoption by single people*, London: BAAF

Parker R. (ed) (1999) *Adoption Now: Messages from research*, Chichester: Wiley

Performance Innovation Unit (2000) *The Prime Minister's Review of Adoption*, London: Performance Innovation Unit

Quinton D. *et al* (forthcoming) *Matching in Adoptions from Care: A conceptual and research review*, London: BAAF

Quinton D., Rushton A., Dance C. and Mayes D. (1998) *Joining New Families: A study of adoption and fostering in middle childhood*, Chichester: John Wiley & Sons

Quinton D. and Selwyn J. (2006) 'Adoption in the UK: outcomes, influences and supports', in McAuley C., Pecora P. J. and Rose W. (eds) *Enhancing the Well-Being of Children and Families through Effective Interventions*, London: Jessica Kingsley Publishers, pp 253–65

Romaine M. with Turley T. and Tuckey N. (2007) *Preparing Children for Permanence*, London: BAAF

Rowe J. and Lambert L. (1973) *Children Who Wait*, London: BAAF

Rushton A. (2000) *Adoption as a Placement Choice: Arguments and evidence*, London: Institute of Psychiatry

Rushton A. (2003) *The Adoption of Looked After Children: A scoping review of research*, London: Social Care Institute for Excellence

Rushton A. and Dance C. (2002a) 'Quality Protects: a commentary on the government's agenda and the evidence base', *Child and Adolescent Mental Health*, 7:2, pp 60–65

Rushton A. and Dance C. (2002b) *Adoption Support Services for Families in Difficulty*, London: BAAF

Rushton A., Dance C., Quinton D. and Mayes D. (2001) *Siblings in Late Permanent Placements*, London: BAAF

Ryan T. and Walker R. (2007) *Life Story Work: A practical guide to helping children understand their past*, London: BAAF

Schofield G. and Beek M. (2006) *Attachment Handbook for Foster Care and Adoption*, London: BAAF

Schofield G., Beek M. and Sargent K. with Thoburn J. (2000) *Growing Up in Foster Care*, London: BAAF

Sellick C., Neil E., Young J., Healey N. and Lorgelli P. (2007) 'An examination of adoption support services for birth relatives and for post-adoption contact in England and Wales', *Adoption & Fostering*, 31:4, pp 17–26

Selwyn J. and Misca G. (2006) *Could it be You? A survey of Barnardo's adopters and foster carers*, Hadley Centre for Adoption and Foster Care Studies (University of Bristol) and Barnardo's Maidenhead, Berkshire: Barnardo's Publications

Selwyn J., Harris P., Quinton D., Nawaz S., Wijedasa D. and Wood M. (2008) *Pathways to Permanence for Black, Asian and Mixed Ethnicity Children: Decisions, dilemmas and outcomes*, Report to the Department for Children, Schools and Families, Bristol: School for Policy Studies, University of Bristol (this study will be published by BAAF in 2010)

Selwyn J., Sempik J., Thurston P. and Wijedasa D. (2009) *Adoption and the Inter-Agency Fee*, Report to the Department for Children, Schools and Families, Hadley Centre for Adoption and Foster Care Studies, Bristol: University of Bristol and Centre for Child and Family Research, Loughborough University

Selwyn J., Sturgess W., Quinton D. and Baxter C. (2006) *Costs and Outcomes of Non-Infant Adoptions*, London: BAAF

Shah S. and Argent H. (2006) *Life Story Work: What it is and what it means*, London: BAAF

Sinclair I. and Wilson K. (2003) 'Matches and mismatches: the contribution of carers and children to the success of foster placements', *British Journal of Social Work*, 33:7, pp 871–84

Smith F. and Stewart R. with Cullen D. (2006) *Adoption Now: Law, regulations, guidance and standards*, London: BAAF

Steele M., Hodges J., Kaniuk J., Henderson K., Hillman S. and Bennett P. (1999a) 'The use of story stem narratives in assessing the inner world of the child: implications for adoptive placements', in Fratter J., Phillips R. and McWilliam E. (eds) *Assessment, Preparation and Support: Implications from research*, London: BAAF, pp 19–29

Steele M., Kaniuk J., Hodges J., Haworth C. and Huss S. (1999b) 'The use of the Adult Attachment Interview: implications for assessment in adoption and foster care', in *Assessment, Preparation and Support: Implications from research*, London: BAAF, pp 30–37

Triseliotis J. (2002) 'Long-term foster care or adoption: the evidence examined', *Child and Family Social Work*, 7:1, pp 23–33

Triseliotis J., Shireman J. and Hundleby M. (1997) *Adoption: Theory, policy and practice*, London: Cassell

Valdez G. M. and McNamara J. R. (1994) 'Matching to prevent adoption disruption', *Child and Adolescent Social Work Journal*, 11, pp 391–403

Valentine D., Conway P. and Randolph J. (1988) 'Placement disruptions: perspectives of adoptive parents', *Journal of Social Work and Human Sexuality*, 6:3, pp 133–53

Ward M. (1997) 'Family paradigms and older-child adoption: a proposal for matching parents' strengths to children's needs', *Family Relations*, 46:3, pp 57–262

# Appendix A

## Participating agencies

We are indebted to the following agencies that took part in the survey and gave permission for their contributions to be acknowledged.

### Local authorities

Barking and Dagenham
Bedfordshire
Blackburn with Darwen
Blackpool
Bournemouth
Bracknell Forest
Brent
Brighton & Hove City
Bristol City
Bromley
Buckinghamshire
Calderdale
Cornwall
Croydon
Cumbria
Derby City
Devon
Dudley
East Riding of Yorkshire
Essex
Gateshead
Gloucestershire
Greenwich
Halton
Hammersmith & Fulham

Hampshire
Hartlepool
Herefordshire
Hertfordshire
Isle of Wight
Kent
Kingston upon Thames
Kirklees
Leeds
Lewisham
Liverpool
Luton
Merton
Middlesbrough
Milton Keynes
Monmouthshire
Neath Port Talbot
Newcastle
Newport City
Norfolk
North Lincolnshire
North Somerset
Northamptonshire
Nottinghamshire
Oxfordshire

Rhondda Cynon Taff
Richmond upon Thames
Rochdale
Solihull
Somerset
South Gloucestershire
South Tyneside
Southampton City
Southwark
Staffordshire
Stockport Metropolitan
Stoke on Trent City
Suffolk
Sunderland City
Surrey
Sutton
Vale of Glamorgan
Walsall
Warwickshire
West Sussex
Westminster City
Wiltshire
Windsor and Maidenhead
Wirral

Families That Last
Families Through Adoption
Manchester Adoption Society
NCH Adoption
NCH Adoption Yorkshire
NCH SW Adoption and Foster Care
Parents And Children Together
SSAFA Forces Help
St Francis' Children's Society
The Together Trust

## Voluntary adoption agencies
Adoption Matters
Barnardo's Cymru
Blackburn Diocesan Adoption Agency
Catholic Children's Rescue Society
Coram Family
Families Are Best
Families For Children Trust

# Appendix B

## Glossary

- **Adoption and Children Act 2002**
  The Adoption and Children Act 2002 (England and Wales) set out the biggest overhaul of adoption law for 26 years. It was designed to improve and modernise the adoption process, including intercountry adoption, and ensure that the needs of the child are paramount. The Act was fully implemented in December 2005.
  (From: www.bemyparent.org.uk/info-for-families/glossary/)

- **Adoption financial support**
  Lump sums or ongoing payments may be made at any stage. All financial support payments are means-tested, so the financial circumstances of adopters have to be assessed. The payment is made by the placing authority.
  (From: www.bemyparent.org.uk/info-for-families/glossary/)

- **Adoption panel**
  An adoption panel is an advisory group, established by the adoption agency or the local authority, which considers applications to be approved as adopters, and recommends whether applicants should be approved.
  Every adoption agency is required by law to have an adoption panel. A maximum of ten people sit on the panel, including:
  - at least two social workers who have at least three years' post-qualifying experience in child care social work, including direct experience in adoption work;
  - at least one registered medical practitioner;
  - at least four other people who are considered by the Secretary of State to be suitable as members including, where reasonably practicable, people with personal experience of adoption.
  (From: www.opsi.gov.uk/)

- **Adoption recommendation or "should be placed for adoption" recommendation**
  This is a recommendation by a local authority's adoption panel that the plan for a child should be for adoption. This recommendation must subsequently be endorsed by the agency's decision maker and the plan then submitted to the court. This terminology replaced the "Best Interest" recommendation after the implementation (in December 2005) of the Adoption and Children Act 2002.

- **BAAF (British Association for Adoption & Fostering)**
  BAAF is a registered charity, involved in family-finding, publications, training, conferences, consultancy, campaigning and advice on all aspects of adoption and fostering.

- **Care order**
  A child may be subject to a care order if the court considers it unsafe for that child to live at home. The child is "looked after" by the local authority, which shares parental responsibility with the child's birth parents. The local authority is responsible for decisions about the child's welfare, including where she or he lives and who she or he has contact with.
  (From: www.bemyparent.org.uk/info-for-families/glossary/)

- **Child's Permanence Report (CPR)**
  This report gives details about a child, his or her family, history, health and particular needs. It is presented to the adoption panel to consider adoption as the placement plan, and is often used as the main source of information about a child in the family-finding process. BAAF has produced a standard format for this report, also called the CPR, which replaced the Form E in 2005.

- **Concurrent planning**
  Concurrent planning is a specialist form of parallel planning where babies and toddlers are placed in foster care and remain with the same carers while efforts are made to reach the primary goal of family reunification. During this period, the children have regular contact

with their birth parents. If reunification fails, the child remains with the same foster family and will be adopted by them.

- **Direct (or face-to-face) contact**
  This involves a meeting or a visit by birth family members or others who are, or have been, significant to a child. With birth family members, the meeting often takes place in a neutral area, such as a family centre, sometimes under the supervision of a social worker.
  (From: www.bemyparent.org.uk/info-for-families/glossary/)

- **Freeing order**
  Under a freeing order, all parental responsibility is transferred from the birth parents to the local authority and the child is "freed" for adoption. Freeing orders were often granted when the birth parents were considered to be unreasonably withholding their consent to their child being adopted. They were replaced by placement orders in December 2005. However, there are still some children under freeing orders who are waiting for a new family.
  (From: www.bemyparent.org.uk/info-for-families/glossary/)

- **Independent Review Mechanism**
  The Independent Review Mechanism (IRM) is a review process conducted by a panel, which prospective adopters can use when they have been told that their adoption agency does not propose to approve them as suitable to adopt a child. It was launched by BAAF on 30 April 2004 on behalf of the Department for Education and Skills (now the Department for Children, Schools and Families) and has now been extended to review cases of prospective foster carers.
  (From www.irm-adoption.org.uk)

- **Indirect (letterbox) contact**
  This may include progress reports, letters, videos or photographs of the child, usually sent or exchanged between the adoptive parents and birth family members through a third party, such as a social worker or an agency.
  (From: www.bemyparent.org.uk/info-for-families/glossary/)

- **Life story work and life story book**
  A life story book is usually prepared with the child by a social worker, foster carer and/or adoptive parent or other carer. The book includes the recording of significant information and events for a child to refer to when they are older or as they grow up, such as a description of their birth family, where they were born, significant people in their lives and their care history. The book may be used to prepare children for an adoptive placement or, for younger children, to help them understand their past as they grow up.
  (From: www.bemyparent.org.uk/info-for-families/glossary/)

- **Linking**
  In this report, linking refers to the process of investigating the suitability of one or more prospective adoptive families who, based on their Prospective Adopter's Report, seem to meet the needs of a certain child or sibling group.

- **"Looked after"**
  A looked after child is "in the care of" or "accommodated by" their local authority, often within a foster family, because their birth parents are temporarily unable to care for them. Most children return to their birth families within a short time but other alternative options, such as adoption or permanent fostering, may be considered to be in their best interests.
  (From: www.bemyparent.org.uk/info-for-families/glossary/)

- **Matching**
  Matching in this report refers to the process whereby a local authority decides which prospective adoptive family is the most suitable family to adopt a certain child or sibling group. This family will be brought forward as a "match" for the child or sibling group at the adoption panel.

- **Parallel planning**
  Parallel planning is the term given to a situation where the plan for a

child is reunification but the elements of planning for an alternative permanent placement are put in place simultaneously, in case the plan to return home is unsuccessful.

- **Placement order**
  A placement order made by the court under Section 21 of the Adoption and Children Act 2002 authorises a local authority to place a child for adoption with any prospective adopters who may be chosen by the authority. It gives a local authority permission to place a child for adoption with or without the birth parents' agreement. Placement orders can be granted when the court decides that adoption is in a child's best interests but the birth parents are unreasonably withholding their consent. Parental responsibility for the child is shared between the local authority, the birth parents and the adoptive parents until the child is legally adopted. Placement orders replaced freeing orders in December 2005.
  (From: www.bemyparent.org.uk/info-for-families/glossary/)

- **Prospective Adopter's Report (PAR) (formerly Form F)**
  This is the report prepared by an adoption agency that gives information about a prospective adoptive family, their health, capacities and support network. The report is presented to the adoption panel to consider the suitability of the prospective adopters to provide a stable home for a child or sibling group.

- **Residence order**
  This is an order under Section 8 of the Children Act 1989 settling the arrangements as to the person(s) with whom the child is to live. Where a residence order is made in favour of someone who does not already have parental responsibility for the child (e.g. a relative or foster carer), that person acquires parental responsibility subject to certain restrictions (e.g. they will not be able to consent to the child's adoption). Parental responsibility given in connection with a residence order will last only as long as the residence order.

- **Service Level Agreement**

  A Service Level Agreement is a formal negotiated agreement between two parties, in this report between local authorities or between a local authority and a voluntary agency. Agencies agree on the services to be provided and the responsibilities of each party. This form of agreement may be used, for example, when adoption support services are outsourced to a specialist agency.

- **Special guardianship**

  Special guardianship provides permanence for children for whom adoption or fostering is not the best option. The special guardian is the child's permanent carer and can exercise parental responsibility to the exclusion of others on most issues. Support services for special guardians are similar to those for adopters. Special guardianship is a new option introduced under the Adoption and Children Act 2002 (England and Wales).

  (From: www.bemyparent.org.uk/info-for-families/glossary/)

- **Voluntary adoption agency**

  A voluntary adoption agency is a registered and inspected adoption agency run by a non-statutory organisation, for example, Barnardo's or NCH. They range in size and often specialise in the type of adoption they offer, for example, they may specifically seek adoptive families for black children or for sibling groups.

  (From: www.bemyparent.org.uk/info-for-families/glossary/)

# Appendix C

## Examples of matching grids

These are examples of two different matching matrices, with thanks to the two local authorities who have given their permission for us to reproduce these documents.

### Warwickshire County Council
### Adoption matching matrix

**Child/ren's name/s**

**Prospective adopters**

| Identified placement needs and requirements | Essential or desirable | Prospective adopter's capacity to meet identified needs |
|---|---|---|
| | | |
| | | |
| | | |
| | | |

**Bristol City Council, Children And Young People's Department**
**Assessment of adoption support needs and matching criteria**

Name of child _____    D.O.B. _____

Date of matching meeting _____

Child's social worker to complete

| | Child's needs including support needs | Family Placement Team workers to complete | | |
| --- | --- | --- | --- | --- |
| | | Family 1 | Family 2 | Family 3 |
| 1 Ethnicity | | | | |
| 2 Culture | | | | |
| 3 Religion | | | | |
| 4 Language | | | | |
| 5 Identity (*life story work/preparation for adoption. Future work needed*) | | | | |
| 6 Emotional needs/attachment difficulties (*current services/anticipated support needs*) | | | | |
| 7 Presenting behaviour (*describe behaviour/ services provided/anticipated support needs*) | | | | |
| 8 Personality | | | | |

| | | | | | | |
|---|---|---|---|---|---|---|
| 9 Health (*current needs/services provided/ anticipated future needs*) | | | | | | |
| 10 Disability (*current needs/services provided/ anticipated support needs*) | | | | | | |
| 11 Education (*current needs/services provided/ anticipated support needs*) | | | | | | |
| 12 Social and family relationships (*child's relationship to birth family (including siblings)/ current carers including men, women and children*) | | | | | | |
| 13 Physical characteristics/ social presentation (*anticipated support needs*) | | | | | | |
| 14 Self-care skills (*current needs/services provided/anticipated support needs*) | | | | | | |
| 15 Interests/hobbies/talents (*include details re: birth parents if applicable*) | | | | | | |
| 16 Child's wishes | | | | | | |
| 17 Birth parents' wishes | | | | | | |
| 18 Contact (*plans for post-adoption/anticipated support needs*) | | | | | | |
| 19 Location and any other practical issues including financial support | | | | | | |
| 20 Potential vulnerabilities/ risks to placement | | | | | | |

# Appendix D

## Explanation of boxplot

Graphic explanation of how to read a boxplot.

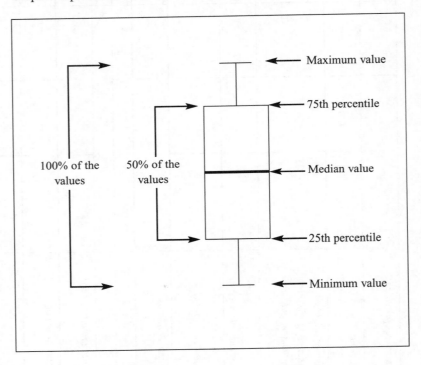

# Index

*Compiled by Elisabeth Pickard*

case-holding responsibility 45–6,
167
chair, of adoption panel 127–8
chemistry, in successful matching
94
Child Adoption Assessment Report
(CAAR) see Child's
Permanence Report (CPR)
Child Appreciation Days 120, 121,
160
child psychologists/psychiatrists 3,
50–1
meeting with adopters 120,
121
childcare experience, in matching
91–2, 105–6
children
and adoption panel meetings
133
adoption preparation 3, 45–54,
154–6
practice variation 54
family-finder meeting 114,
157–8
family finding, timeliness 41–2
information given to adopters
118–22
input to profile 66
linking to families 70–6
matching
characteristics in 5–6, 101,
102
expectations in 117
key factors in 87–90
*Children Who Wait* (Adoption UK)
4–5
children with behavioural problems
104–6
children with disabilities 154
adopter recruitment 2, 3, 56–7
data issues 36–7
placement delay 14, 15
placing with siblings 110, 111

children with special needs
data issues 36–7
issues in matching 102–3
placement issues 104–6
children's assessments 3, 45–54,
154–6
accuracy and completeness
87–90
costs of 145, 146, 166
practice variation 53–4
time taken 48–51
tools and approaches 49–52
children's needs, in matching 161,
162
children's profiles 66–8, 157–9
costs of 145, 147, 166
dissemination 4–5, 71, 72, 73,
74–5, 168–9
elusive characteristics in 16–17
showing the "whole child"
15–16
children's views/wishes 94–5,
159
Child's Permanence Report (CPR)
46–7, 154
information given to adopters
119
in linking 70
in matching 7, 114, 160
quality of 130, 162
consortia activities
inter-agency fees 76–8
in linking 71, 72, 73
placements made 153
contact plans (post-adoption)
issue in matching 93, 95, 96,
101, 161, 163
professional views on 110,
111
costs
of adoption activities 17–18,
136–51, 165–6
barrier to matching 6, 95

in-house placements 2, 153
  family finders and 114
  frequency 37–8
  mechanisms for linkage 70–6
Independent Review Mechanism
  (IRM) 132
information
  for prospective adopters
    118–22, 160
  quality of 161–2
  scrutiny by adoption panel
    128–32
instrument development 20–1
inter-agency fees 17–18, 143,
  144
  barrier to matching 6
  hard-to-place children
    163–4
  budget constraints and 76–80
  comparative data 76–80
inter-agency placements 2
  frequency of 37–8, 71–6
  issues in 78–80
  time costs 148–9
internet, in linking 72, 73–4

kinship placements 46

Life Appreciation Days 120, 121,
  160
life story books 119–20, 160
life story work 52
linking 70–6, 157–9
  costs of 145, 147–9, 166
  defined 1, 12
  information for adopters
    118–22
  professionals' views on 103–12
  tools and approaches 122–4
local authorities
  administrative categories 33
  adopters' post-approval
    timescale 63, 65

adoption team sizes 33–4
characteristics in study 32–44
English 25–7
participating/non-participating
  characteristics 25–7
on professional-led matching
  108–9
proportion of looked-after
  children adopted 25–7
rates of approval for adoptive
  families 40
salary costs 142–4
staffing profile 138–40
study sample 23
unit costs on adoption services
  145–9
Welsh 28–9
see also costs; inter-agency
  placements
looked after children, adoption rates
  25–9, 32–3

marginal costs 137n
matching 6–7, 98–9, 114–25,
  159–61
  barriers to 6, 89, 95–8, 162
  expectations of adopters
    93
  costs of 111–12, 145, 148–9
  criteria, relaxation of 69
  defined 1, 12
  developments in 164
  information shared with
    adopters 118–22
  issues in 101–13, 161–4
  key factors 86–100, 124–5
  meetings held 115–18
  priorities 101–13, 161–4
  professionals' views on 103–12
  service operation in 87–90
  time spent by adoption panel
    128–32
  timeliness of placement 109–10